The Elephant Who Walked to Manchester

by

David Barnaby

Basset Publications
Plymouth

Acknowledgements

Thanks to the Zoological Society of Greater Manchester for providing a discipline and framework for this and other projects. Thanks to Anthony Marlow for assistance with research in Edinburgh, Manchester and towns on the route, and for proof reading and text criticism: to Clinton Keeling for encouragement and for C J Cornish; to Dr M V Hounsome, Keeper of Zoology at the University Museum of Manchester; to Michael Powell and the Librarians at Chetham's Library, Manchester; to Mr Meredith of Hyde for "Lorenzo" the musical composition; to Norman Marlow for railway expertise; to Susan and Fred Baker for hospitality while researching; and to V J A Manton, Curator at Whipsnade, for responding. The help of the librarians at the central reference library, Manchester; Central Library and Scottish National Library, Edinburgh; and the central reference libraries in Bolton, Preston, Lancaster, Carlisle and Hawick is also acknowledged, with particular thanks to Christine Strickland of Kendal Library. Thanks to Chris Moiser, who also responded.

Cover: *The Disputed Toll* courtesy of the University Museum of Manchester.

First published August 1988

I.S.B.N. 0 946873 96 8

Published by Basset Publications, North Hill, Plymouth, S. Devon.

Printed by The Western Litho Company of Plymouth, Heather House, Gibbon Lane, Plymouth, Devon.

CONTENTS

The map shows the route of the walk taken by Lorenzo and Maharajah. Lorenzo, as a man experienced with travelling menageries, would probably know which towns to head for to make up the most direct route.

Lorenzo Lawrence –
Forty years at the Gardens circa 1912

Courtesy of Chethams Library

Chapter 1

Spring 1872

Up to the middle of April people had considered the weather to be rather cold for the time of year; a North-East wind had been blowing and driving clouds of dust along the highways. The new Spring growth in the fields and in the gardens was a little slow in coming but not seriously retarded. The weather had not been so bad that work and play out of doors was prevented or even unpleasant. It was a typically changeable English Spring. The migrant birds, arriving for the Summer, were remarkably early. In fact, the Swallows seemed to be so early around Carlisle that the Carlisle Journal wondered if they had left Britain for the Winter at all. They had been seen near Lancaster on the eleventh of April, the same day on which a Nightingale had been heard near Sandhurst. In Bromley, however, Nightingales had been singing since the second, where they had never been heard before the fourteenth. A Cuckoo was heard near Workington on the thirteenth and another, near Orton, on the fifteenth.

Ten garotters, convicted at Leeds assizes, were thrashed with the cat o' nine tails at Armley gaol. A man in Preston put his wife on the fire; she died soon afterwards in hospital.

The government decided to call in the fourpenny pieces because confusion was arising from having two coins of nearly the same value and appearance.

David Livingstone was somewhere in Africa, trying to trace the sources of the Nile, but there had recently been no reliable news about him. He was presumed dead by certain major agencies of news. Lloyd's agents at Zanzibar had no information.

Paris was in the early stages of recovery from the Franco-Prussian War. The Jardin des Plantes, the zoological garden, had been seriously depleted in animals as everything edible had provided food for the Parisians.

Charles Darwin's new book this year would be "The Expression of Emotions in Man and Animals". Last year it had been "The Descent of Man". His bestseller, "The Origin of Species", was still creating waves but had now been available for thirteen years and would go into a sixth edition during the year.

Entertainment was live and alive. On the nineteenth of April, during a performance at the New Gaiety Theatre in West Hartlepool, a female Japanese performer belonging to "The Great Dragon Troupe" fell forty feet from a steeply inclined rope which she was ascending from the stage to the gallery. She was about six feet from the top when a man struck a vesuvian just before her eyes. After landing in the audience she went back to the stage and completed her performance. No-one in the audience was badly hurt.

In O'Brien's Menagerie in America, a keeper called Whittle transferred to the Lion act. While rehearsing with the Lion in an inn yard with a few spectators, Whittle, still unaccustomed to working with Lions, put his head in the Lion's mouth. The Lion, still unaccustomed to working with Whittle, closed its jaws. Whittle was later in a critical condition.

The Zoological Gardens in London, about forty years old, the first of their kind and open every day except Sunday, were advertising a "Hairy Rhinoceros from Chittagong, never before exhibited". Zoological history of another kind was also made during the year at Regent's Park; its significance perhaps not fully realised. The female Quagga – a kind of zebra which is part brown and part striped – died. She was the only zoo Quagga ever to be photographed. The last ever Quagga in the wild was already dead; it had been killed two years before. It cost one shilling to go into London Zoo but only sixpence on a Monday.

Zoological Gardens on permanent sites were a growth industry. After London; Dublin, Bristol and Manchester had been soon on the scene. Manchester's Belle Vue was at least as popular for its truly spectacular firework 'pictures' as for its animals, but its zoological collection was nevertheless significant and widely respected.

A prospectus for the new Manchester Aquarium Company could be obtained from the District Bank. The aquarium was to be established in Whalley Range on a site now occupied by a school.

Sixty animals, sent by the late Lord Mayo, were on their way from Calcutta to the Zoological Gardens in Dublin.

Travelling menageries were a more established medium of entertainment and unwitting education. They were almost as exciting to see moving in procession from town to town as when they set up their exhibition.

Just why a famous menagerie called "Wombwell's Royal

Number One" should be owned by a man called Alexander Fairgrieve will be explained in a later chapter. Mr Fairgrieve decided to retire in the Spring of 1872. He sold all the horses (used for pulling the numerous waggons) early in the year and arranged a spectacular auction – a show in itself – of all the menagerie animals, waggons and gear for the month of April. The auction was to be in Edinburgh, Mr Fairgrieve's own town and the place to which he planned to retire.

Chapter 2

Wombwell's

An elephant walking the highways of Britain was a much more common sight in the nineteenth century than in the twentieth. Such an elephant, most usually a part of a travelling menagerie, would generate local interest but would not be regarded as nationally newsworthy.

In the second half of the twentieth century, the meaning of the word 'menagerie' has become somewhat debased in certain circles. It is used to mean all that is bad about animal husbandry. It was not always so; until the word 'zoo' was coined (to refer exclusively to London Zoo), 'menagerie' was the normal unemotional term for a collection of animals, usually one which people could go and see. The word 'zoo' itself, never a noble word, may follow 'menagerie' into the politico-emotive arena. Be that as it may, travelling menageries were an accepted part of nineteenth-century life. There were good ones and bad ones, big ones and small ones, famous ones visited by royalty and shameful ones exploiting the baser human qualities. They were visited by savants and labourers alike, each seeking to see creatures that they could not see elsewhere. The menageries travelled from town to town in a train of waggons pulled by horses, and played a major role in the calendar of town events. The larger animals, such as Camels and Elephants, often made the journeys on foot, and the whole procession was reminiscent, in the popular mind, of the fabulous parade of animals into Noah's Ark. The biblical Noah and his animals had been very high in the public consciousness since Darwin had published 'The Origin of Species'' in 1859. Noah's Ark as a children's toy was so popular at this period that it has become a classic. The big fierce animals might be seen occupying the rolling cages as the procession passed if the weather was fine. These cages usually had wooden shutters which would protect the occupants from bad weather and keep the animals from public view for business reasons or for the sake of the animals at times of sickness or pregnancy, or if they simply did not thrive on the public gaze en route.

The rate of travelling depended very much on the state of the roads, but averaged two miles an hour.

The living waggons (waggons in which people lived) were usually of a size to be pulled by a single Horse and were about twelve feet long. George Wombwell's own living waggon was twenty feet long and drawn by three Horses. It was built of solid mahogany and had cost the immense sum of £850. Wombwell's stage waggon needed six horses to pull it. It was twenty feet long but opened to fifty-four feet.

Wombwell's was not the first of the major travelling menageries, although it was among the earliest. The Wombwell name, however, was destined to become the most famous of all in Britain, and the several menageries which later had a right to use the name guarded the privilege fiercely.

The heart and essence of any menagerie was, of course, its collection of exotic creatures, but, like any equivalent in the twentieth century, be it zoological garden, safari park or museum of natural history, it was always ready to have other exhibits loosely peripheral to the zoological centre. The British Empire was at its height. Treasures ethnological, anthropological and biological, and exotica of all kinds were flooding into the country. The menageries, along with the young zoological gardens, botanical gardens, and numerous large private collections, played their part in exhibiting the material. The menageries were as 'educational' in their way as many a more august institution. Some people just gawped, guffawed, sniggered and dribbled; others learned from the experience. The same is true today in the best of zoological gardens, wildlife reserves or museums. Those menageries which, today, we would class as the less reputable, were quite happy to exhibit freaks, including human ones, under the broadened umbrella of exotica. The labelling and naming of the rarer animals and more unusual freaks was often a credit to the flexibility of the human imagination.

The story of George Wombwell's enterprise has been briefly told in several books. George was born in Essex in 1777. Fascinated by the exotic creatures brought back on ships coming up the Thames, he began to acquire some of the creatures for himself. The turning point seems to have come when he acquired two large Common Boas (Boa Constrictors), the first recorded ones ever imported into Britain. He paid £75 for them, exhibited them for a small entrance fee and more than recouped his investment within three weeks.

George Wombwell and those who followed him in the business were never afraid to invest. Very early in his career George paid £800 for two Giraffes, spent an immense amount on their accommodation and lost heavily when they both died within a very short time. Not long afterwards he paid £2000 for a further four Giraffes but all of them died within four months. He was also responsible for the purchase of the first Rhinoceros ever imported into Britain. The menageries did not import their own animals; they purchased those imported by others. The menageries were the pioneers – with all that that word implies – in the husbandry of exotic animals and in popular education about them. They worked within the knowledge and aspirations of their times. That knowledge has now increased (the menageries themselves added much) and some of the aspirations have changed.

The Wombwell Menagerie could look backwards as well as forwards. In 1825, in the very early days, George arranged for an exhibition fight between Lions and Dogs. What he had done, in fact, was to wager his Lions against the bulldogs of some 'sporting' gentleman. The Dogs would undoubtedly have destroyed larger animals many times before. The first Lion in the arena – it took place in Warwick – simply would not fight. It is hardly surprising. He was a very tame and gentle animal. The public could actually pay twopence to go into his cage. He would even allow people to ride on his back. He was one of several generations of Lions to be called Nero. Wallace, the second Lion, who was also to have many namesakes, was then faced by the six Dogs and he killed them all. In 1825, it must be remembered, bull baiting, Badger baiting and cockfighting were common entertainments. Many people would have it so today. This Lion-baiting event was recalled by one or two newspapers when they reported the auction of Alexander Fairgrieve's 'Wombwell's Number One' in 1872. They also recalled how, in 1851, one of George's nieces, known professionally as The Lion Queen, giving in to the persuasions of some visitors, went one day into a Tigers' cage where the animals were excited by feeding. She was killed in typical Tiger fashion – seized by the neck. The Tiger knew her, however, and immediately let her go. She died almost immediately afterwards with very little external injury. Present-day keepers might not be urged to do such things by the public but they have certainly fallen into the same trap when tempted by television and film cameras.

The husbandry of exotic animals was an art in a state of clumsy infancy at the end of the eighteenth century. (It had doubtless reached stages of greater refinement in other civilisations). The menageries and a rapidly developing 'profession' of keepers did much to develop the infant. Menageries were undoubtedly show business and keepers were often showmen and performers as well. Show business has always attracted the inadequates, the boasters and the seekers of fame, quick fortune and attention, but it has always contained a proportion of true artists. The profession of animal keeping is no exception.

George Wombwell's menagerie soon went on the road. Everyone directly concerned; George himself, his wife and relatives, keepers, drivers, musicians, and so on, lived and moved with the menagerie.

George was known as a man of considerable determination and courage. He was widely known and respected. He was prepared to enter the cage of any animal he possessed and, perhaps establishing a tradition among dedicated keepers, got in beside any animal when it was sick, and administered the medicine. The usual medicine was that universal cure-all for Lions, Monkeys, Cattle or human beings – castor oil. He wore only the finest linen ruffled shirts and would never wear a pair of boots which had been mended, and the ones that he did wear had to be scrupulously clean and gleaming. For the rest of his dress, however, he was totally careless. His wardrobe, boots and shirts apart, was reputed to be worth less than five shillings at the time of his death.

George married but had no children. Mrs Wombwell managed the finances and there was one stretch of twenty years during which she never left the menagerie, even for one night. Unlike Mr Fairgrieve, George never retired. When he died, it was in the mahogany living van in which he lived and travelled with the menagerie (by then known as Number One). He was seventy-three years old at his death. He was buried in Highgate Cemetery.

By the time George died in 1850 there were three Wombwell's menageries. They operated quite separately and were known simply as Number One, Number Two and Number Three. Wombwell's Royal Number One Menagerie was, of course, the original, and the one which happens to concern us most in this story.

George had launched himself as a full-time menagerist (he had been a shoe maker) in 1805. When his collection filled fourteen waggons the time had come to form Number Two. By this stage, travelling menageries were widely popular and he had several serious rivals in the field. On one occasion, when he was on business in London, George realised that Atkins' Menagerie was about to upstage him at St Bartholomew's Fair, at Smithfield. His own menagerie was in Newcastle on Tyne. He immediately travelled

North (by horse power) and had his fourteen waggons, nearly sixty horses (twelve of which pulled the thirty foot long Elephant waggon) on the way to London. They were in time for the fair, but his Elephant was dead. Atkins immediately advertised his own Elephant as "The Only Living Elephant in the Fair". Within hours Wombwell's big sign read "Come and See the Only Dead Elephant in the Fair". The public did. The crowds had to be held back with barricades and one of the many Wombwell legends was created.

Wombwell was able to include the word 'Royal' in his title because on five occasions his menageries One and Two had had royal visitors. Both One and Two were each twice invited to exhibit for the Royal family in Windsor Castle between 1834 and 1854 (nearly always in October – was this a Royal youngster's birthday?). And in October 1869 the Number One was visited by the Royal family at Ballater, six miles from Balmoral Castle. It is interesting to note that on one occasion in Windsor some hybrid Lion-Tiger cubs were viewed and handled by Her Majesty. By now George Wombwell was a national figure.

The first Wombwell menagerie to be sold off after George's death in 1850 was Number Three. Because George had no children the three menageries were left to various other members of his family. Number Two was left to a niece called Mrs Edmonds. It was this one which was destined to survive the longest and, under Bostock management, to subdivide into a further three menageries. George's widow took over Number One. So only one of the three menageries was left to a man, and that was to be the least successful. Mrs Wombwell managed Number One for fifteen years and its reputation grew. Her own nephew, Alexander Fairgrieve, took over from her on January 1st 1865 and continued the work as well as ever. 'The Scotsman' reported that almost every animal exhibited, except the elephant and rhinoceros, had bred within the show. Certainly, no less than nine camel calfs had been born and raised while Mr Fairgrieve was proprietor. Some of these young camels were hybrids – crossed between Bactrian Camels and Dromedaries. Several lions, too, had their parents within the menagerie.

The menagerie employed about forty men, and had a permanent corps of at least as many horses whose main job was the hauling of the numerous waggons. There were fifteen horse keepers whose duties were to look after the horses and to act as drivers. There were twelve 'inside' men who looked after all interior matters and attended to the animals. Responsibility for the animals was in the hands of two head keepers. These two trained the animals as well as seeing them well fed, watered, housed and exercised. Another key person was the inspector of waggons.

There were then ten musicians and a doorkeeper. One member of the menagerie, known as the agent, always travelled some weeks ahead of the show to make the necessary arrangements for the site, the stabling, publicity and so on.

One of the problems faced by the more enlightened twentieth-century zoos has been that certain species of animals can live tedious existences even when accommodated in de-luxe housing. For all the perceived faults of the travelling menageries, their animals are unlikely to have led barren lives consisting of empty days. In many cases, their keepers actually lived with them and creatures such as elephants frequently had work to do in the moving of waggons and equipment, both on site and travelling.

Many individual animals, as well as keepers/performers, were nationally famous, and could be referred to by name in newspapers with little difficulty. The keeper called Mr Lawrence, for example, was very widely known under his show-business name of Lorenzo the Lion Tamer, with little need for further explanation. One black-maned lion (the modern safari-park public still prefers black-maned lions) called Hannibal was acknowledged to be the finest lion in Britain. His fellows, Boss and Wallace were equally well-known.

There were two elephants in Mr Fairgrieve's menagerie. They were both Asian. There was a young female and a rather splendid male. The female was reputed to be a competent player of the organ, presumably with her trunk. The male was about seven and a half feet tall and had an impressive pair of twenty-inch tusks. He was about eight years old, growing fast, intelligent and known as an exceedingly clever – and docile – performing elephant. One of his jobs was to pull the band waggon. He worked quite willingly in harness. He would push or pull a waggon up a hill, would work in a team with any horses (he had the front position), and used to place all the waggons in their correct positions with only two men to guide the wheels. He was later to be known as Maharajah, and may well have been then, although he was occasionally given other names by the press.

For a period of his life Maharajah had an iron bar fixed across his tusks, from the tip of one to the tip of the other. This might have rendered him a little less dangerous if he was in a bad mood, although, as we have already noted, he was a particularly good-natured elephant. The bar must have been a terrible inconvenience to him. It has been reasonably assumed by several writers that the bar was fixed by Wombwell's and that Lorenzo, or someone else, used it for show purposes as a sort of gymnastic bar. There is no record at all of Maharajah's bar at this period, however. The newspapers described almost every aspect of Maharajah's appearance and behaviour at the time of the Edinburgh auction, but not one reporter mentioned a bar. Contrary to conventional assumptions, then, it may have been attached after he had left Wombwell's. We do not know. What we do know is that it later appeared in a painting, was then removed, and still exists somewhere in Canada.

The horses and the animal collection devoured an immense amount of food. The carnivorous animals required about four hundredweight of meat daily, consisting mainly of bullocks' shins, hearts and heads. Lions and tigers had about 12lbs of flesh each day and leopards 5lbs. The bears were fed on bread and sop with a piece of flesh on cold days. The monkeys had rice, bread, sop and fruits. The antelopes and cattle were fed much the same as the horses.

The menagerie was not a circus. Its main purpose was to exhibit animals. There was sometimes an extra charge to the public to witness feeding time, and the routine did include some performances. Lorenzo regularly enacted 'Androcles and the Lion' with the lions Hannibal, Boss and others, and there is very little doubt that he enjoyed impressing the public. Lorenzo turned out to be something of an exceptional person in his relationships with animals, but that would not stop him playing his role of Lorenzo the Lion Tamer as a young man enjoying some fame and adulation.

When the menagerie was in the more remote areas, people thought nothing of walking twenty miles or so, to be sure of experiencing it.

The menageries were business. They needed vast amounts of money, not only for daily needs but to provide for the whole life of the owner and the long-term employees. Nevertheless, in the days of child labour and before compulsory schooling, they did serve an undoubted educational purpose – unwitting, perhaps, at first, but later acknowledged in the appointment of 'travelling schoolmasters', the forerunners of present-day zoo education officers.

Mr Fairgrieve worked hard on his reputation as an educator, and he was generally acknowledged as providing a service as well as entertainment.

Chapter 3

The Edinburgh Auction

Alexander Fairgrieve had decided that 1872 would be the year of his retirement. He had arranged for his Number One menagerie to be in Edinburgh from January, and in the early weeks of that year all the horses were sold off. The menagerie would remain stationary – as a sort of zoo, in fact – and the management would be relieved of the maintenance of the non-working horses.

The whole menagerie – animals, equipment and waggons – was to be sold by auction over two days. On the first day all the animals would be sold and on the second day all the waggons and equipment. The dates were to be the 9th and 10th of April. The place was to be the New Vegetable Market in the Pavilion of the Waverley Market, and the auctioneer, Mr R Buist, a man experienced in the sale of natural history objects and exotica.

Because Wombwell's Number One was probably the best known of a group of already famous menageries, the sale attracted a lot of newspaper publicity both before the event and immediately afterwards. The papers took the opportunity of publishing historical résumés of the Wombwell menageries, George himself and allied subjects.

'The Field' and 'The Times' recalled a previous sale of wild animals when the collection of Mr Cross was sold at the Surrey Zoological Gardens. This particular collection of animals had had an equally interesting history. It had been a stationary exhibition in the Strand in a building always known as the Exeter 'Change. It was here that a famous elephant named Chunee was clumsily executed when he was "mad with toothache". The collection was afterwards exhibited at the King's mews, Charing Cross (on the site of the present National Gallery) and later removed to the Surrey Zoological Gardens from where it was dispersed under the hammer of another natural-history auctioneer, a Mr J C Stevens. 'The Field' was interested to compare the 'value' of the two collections as represented by the selling prices.

The sale was unprecedented in Edinburgh both in the nature of the articles for sale and in the amount of excitement it generated. 'The Scotsman' called it "one of the most remarkable sales ever witnessed in Great Britain".

At the Waverley Market, the morning of the 9th of April was occupied with final preparations. A large crowd gathered to watch and were quite happy to pay the half-crown entrance fee. (it would take several pounds today to buy what half a crown would buy in 1872.) Mr Buist mounted the rostrum at a quarter past twelve (although one paper said it was one o'clock) and the end of Wombwell's Royal Number One Menagerie had begun.

The sight of an auctioneer knocking down Lions, Tigers, Elephants, White and Brown Bears, Hyenas, Jackals, Wolves, Monkeys and an absolutely splendid collection of birds was as good a show as Wombwell's had ever put on.

The Edinburgh crowds were there, but so, too, were the top men in the zoological world, at least, the ones who were interested in living animals. The most famous of these was Mr Jamrach.

Jamrach's was in London, not too far from the Tower. The firm had existed since before the turn of the eighteenth century. It occupied the oldest building in a very old street called George Street, formerly known as Ratcliffe Highway. Jamrach's existed when lions were still kept in the Tower and was close to the docks, from which it drew its never-ending supply of exotic objects and animals; birds, mammals, reptiles, armour, weapons, idols, mummies, skulls, skins and thousands of other things which naturalist dealers would acquire. It was an old and curious place with a shop front displaying the objects, and a window full of brightly coloured parrots. The office at the back was where Mr Jamrach did business, first with the ships' captains and then with men such as Frank Buckland, Abraham Bartlett, Carl Hagenbeck, Van Amburgh and any number of other circus and menagerie proprietors and private zoological breeders and collectors. Frank Buckland was a prolific writer on zoological matters, had an amazing houseful of exotic creatures and was an expert on fish and rivers. He would buy from Jamrach for himself, for the Zoological Gardens (i.e. London Zoo) or on behalf of others. Abraham Bartlett was the powerful Superintendent (Head Keeper, in modern equivalent) at the Zoological Gardens. Carl Hagenbeck of Hamburg virtually invented the 'modern' zoo and was the first to organise serious animal-collecting expeditions. Mr Van Amburgh had three big travelling menageries in America. Van Amburgh once purchased from Jamrach's a leopard. After removing it from its box he produced a steel chain and collar from his greatcoat pocket, put the leopard on the chain, got into a cab and continued his business in London.

The zoo business was beginning to boom in America as well as in Europe. Mr Jamrach was a busy man. The spoils of the sea captains were important. The animal trade route out of Africa was blocked in the Sudan by the muslim fanatics, and only Carl Hagenbeck went to get his own animals.

There were a thousand stories from Jamrach's. The place featured in the writings of Charles Dickens. C. J. Cornish, the contemporary writer, observed that Jamrach's always dealt in objects which were about to disappear before the advance of civilisation.

If Mr Jamrach had a rival it was Mr Rice, also of London. He, too, was in Edinburgh for the auction, and was destined to be the major purchaser.

William Cross, already mentioned in connection with the Exeter 'Change and the Surrey Gardens, travelled from Liverpool. He was as well known as the others and was the major naturalist dealer operating in the North of England.

Van Amburgh, known as the Prince of the American Menagerists (the king presumably being Mr Barnum), was not in Edinburgh in person. He sent a Mr Ferguson as his representative.

A certain Professor Edwards travelled to Edinburgh from Paris. The Jardin des Plantes, once exactly what its name implied but now a public zoological garden, was in a rather sorry state. The Sieges of Paris following the Franco-Prussian war had ended only a year before. Most of the zoo animals, and lots of others including cats and rats, had ended their days on the shelves of the butchers' shops. In Paris on New Year's Eve 1871, one butcher was offering, among other unusual heads and joints, the trunk of a young elephant named Pollux, elephant sausages and camel steaks. (The idea of elephant sausages was soon to be raised in Edinburgh.) Professor Edwards was hoping that the Edinburgh auction would help to re-stock the Jardin des Plantes. His purchases were not numerous but they did include a Polar Bear. Some large sums of money changed hands in Edinburgh on 9th April. It is perhaps reasonable to assume that Professor Edwards did not have excessive funds at his disposal from war-torn Paris.

The zoological garden in Bristol, the second oldest in Britain and still today a zoological institution of considerable importance, was represented at the sale by Mr Jackson.

Day's Menagerie, Symonds' Menagerie, Edmonds' Menagerie and Bostock's Menagerie (the last two both descendants of the original Wombwell's) had buyers there, and among the private collectors was a man representing the Earl of Roseberry.

Another of the major zoological figures was James Jennison of Manchester. James was one of the sons of John Jennison who founded Britain's fourth oldest zoological garden in the 1830s. The zoo was Belle Vue in the Gorton area of Manchester. Belle Vue and Jennison enthusiasts like to point out that John's earlier venture in Stockport actually pre-dated the London Zoo. The Jennison family were to own and operate Belle Vue during its most famous years, and well into the twentieth century. Various members of the family contributed in different ways to the development of the city. We do not know if James Jennison had any particular animals in mind before the sale, but he did make at least one memorable purchase.

Mr Buist announced to the crowds that the sale was to be without reserve and then began business in earnest.

The monkeys came up first. Mr Buist recommended them as pets for the drawing room and for the kitchen. He described them as lively, frisky, intelligent, clean, beautiful and half able to speak. Bidding was brisk and competitive. One of the briskest bidders throughout the whole sale was Mr Cross, although he did not take much away with him in the end. A Mandrill went for thirty pounds and a baboon for ten pounds ten shillings. A Tasmanian Devil went to Mrs Day's menagerie for sixty-five shillings. Under what circumstances had **he** travelled to Britain? Years later, the Tasmanian Devil, an animal that few people would recognise if they saw one, actually became a popular film cartoon character in American productions. A most unlikely choice, one would have thought.

Mr Buist and the British public were not sentimental about animals. They admired and valued them according to a variety of criteria. They lived much closer to them than we do today. They lived as close to horses as we do to motor cars. Bidding was slow on the Black Vulture. Mr Buist assured the audience that the bird was worth a guinea for his plumage alone, and a further sovereign to eat afterwards – as long as you cared for roast vulture. It is worth remembering that one of the original aims of the Zoological Society of London had been to acclimatise exotic animals to live and breed in Britain, not only to add variety to our landscape but to our menus as well. There was a certain fashion for eating the flesh of exotic animals. Frank Buckland, for example, never missed an opportunity to acquire the meat of almost any unusual specimen recently dead. Mr Rice paid fifty shillings for the vulture.

Bidding for the Emu was also a little slow. Mr Buist suggested the bird as the basis for a new business in Ostrich farming. Did he know an Emu is not an Ostrich? In any case, one would have thought that at least two birds were necessary to start a farm. The 'emeu', as it was spelt in the catalogue, went to Mrs Day for seven pounds, which was not a bad price in the end. Most of the cockatoos and other parrots went to local collectors and fanciers, and were sold briskly. One 'Lemon Crested Cockatoo' fetched the outstanding sum of eight pounds. This exceptional price was due to the bird's talking ability.

Mr Jamrach bought a pair of Pelicans which had formerly lived in Lancashire on the Earl of Derby's estate near Liverpool. The estate now contains Knowsley Safari Park but that is only the most recent of several zoological collections there. The nineteenth-century collections of the Earl of Derby were significant indeed. The writer Edward Lear, was often a guest there. Lear, incidentally, was a gifted painter of birds in his early adulthood. There are those who consider him the greatest bird painter that Britain has produced.

A Condor who had been with Wombwell's for forty years got fifteen pounds from Mr Rice.

Mr Buist recommended the Ocelot especially to the owners of small shows. It had, he said, all the beauty of the Tiger and Leopard but could be bought for an old song and was perfect for a magnificent large picture for the outside of the show – rather condescending to the Ocelot, perhaps, but a lot less insulting than the indiscriminate twentieth-century killing of Ocelots for their skins. Mr Ferguson paid six pounds ten shillings and added it to the Van Amburgh menageries along with three "fretful" Porcupines which Mr Buist sold while joking about Shakespeare.

With the same lack of sentiment that he had shown over the vulture, Mr Buist said that a local hairdresser had expressed interest in the bears. Professor Edwards, however, had a more serious intent and paid forty pounds for a Polar Bear. Mr Jamrach took a Tibetan Sun Bear for five guineas and Mr Bostock a Brown Bear for seven pounds.

The sale of the bears began that part of the show which had attracted the crowds – the big spectacular mammals; lions, tigers, elephants and bears. It was also the time when the big sums of money would change hands. Mr Jamrach moved on from his five-guinea bear to paying sixty pounds for three leopards which were described as performing animals, and he then proceeded to acquire the first real star of the show, a magnificent female tiger (performing) named Tippoo. He paid a hundred and fifty five pounds. Tippoo was pregnant. Her mate, Poonah, equally beautiful, would probably have fetched even more but he had died only a week before, after catching a cold.

Then Mr Rice became the dominant purchaser. He bought Duke of Edinburgh, a three year old lion, and Nero, a very fine seven year old lion for one hundred and forty pounds each, two young lionesses for eighty pounds each and two young lions, brothers, sons of Hannibal (still to be sold) for ninety pounds each.

The sale of the lions was perhaps the climax of the show. Mr Lawrence – Lorenzo the Lion Tamer – was in attendance and put many of the performing animals through their paces for the benefit of the buyers and the crowd. He offered to go in with the Lions but his offer was declined. Wallace came up for sale. It was with Wallace and Boss that Lorenzo had thrilled many a crowd with his 'Androcles and the Lion' performance. Wallace was seven and a half years old. Mr Rice paid eighty pounds for him.

Poor old Boss, three years old, was described as "faulty". He had an injured eye. Mr Buist recommended him to Edinburgh shopkeepers as an arresting window display. Mr Jamrach paid twenty pounds for him.

The Lion, Hannibal, was a household name. He was a magnificent, black-maned six and a half year old, "the finest and largest in Britain". He was the father of several young Lions in the menagerie. Victoria, a Lioness bought by Mr Jennison, was pregnant by him. Frank Buckland, writing a few days before the sale, maintained that Hannibal really ought to go to the Zoological Gardens in London, even if it meant a small sacrifice on someone's part, as there was no animal to compare with him anywhere in Britain. Abraham Bartlett at the zoo, Buckland's friend, was of the same opinion. Neither Buckland nor Bartlett, as it happened, attended the auction.

The bidding for Hannibal started at fifty pounds and rose slowly to two hundred and twenty-five. Mr Buist said he was ashamed of such a ridiculously small price for the finest lion in the world, and he was sure that Hannibal was as disgusted as he was, and would turn his back on the crowd. Sure enough, and exactly on cue, Hannibal did at that moment deliberately turn round. The crowd was amused. The bidding became lively. The crowd seemed to take Hannibal's disgust at face value. I think we can assume a bit of collusion and that Lorenzo was not far away. Whatever the cause, the finest lion in the land went to Bristol Zoo when Mr Jackson bid two hundred and seventy pounds.

The two elephants, for some reason, fetched disappointing sums. The small female, famous for playing the organ, whistling and firing off cannons, was clearly a financial loss to Mr Fairgrieve. Fairgrieve had paid six hundred pounds for her to Mr Rice some time before. She was still only five feet six inches tall. At the Edinburgh auction Mr Rice bought her back for one hundred and forty-five.

Maharajah was as popular as Hannibal. He was a fine specimen of a male Asian Elephant. Wombwell's never exaggerated his height at seven feet six inches. His skeleton is still with us and can be measured. He had a superb pair of tusks nearly twenty inches long. He was renowned for his intelligence, his docility, his performing ability and his fine form. He was nearly eight years old and not yet fully grown. He had been with Wombwell's since he was five feet high, a period of about four years.

The bidding for Maharajah rested for a time at three hundred and eighty pounds. This was no price for a top-class elephant. Mr Buist, quick and skilful as ever, named a prominent Edinburgh butcher who might invest in the elephant and introduce elephant sausages to Scotland. There must have been others besides Professor Edwards whose minds went back to poor Pollux. The thought of elephant sausages, aided by Mr Buist's skill, quickened the bidding. James Jennison bid six hundred and eighty pounds and Maharajah was destined for Belle Vue, Manchester. The price was easily the highest at the sale for a single animal but it was not outstanding for a tusked specimen like this one. Mr Fairgrieve had paid a comparable amount for the female when she was a baby.

The sale of the animals was over by four o'clock in the afternoon. Mr Buist prepared to return next day to sell the waggons and equipment. The newspapers decided that the sale had been an excellent one and that while certain animals had drawn less than expected, others had drawn more than their market value and that prices had ranged good throughout. Like the elephants, the camels were among the prize exhibits of the menagerie and had been slightly disappointing in the sale. One of the last animals to be sold was a mastiff which had won first prize at a recent show in Edinburgh. He brought the rather high price of twelve pounds. In total, the animals had fetched about two thousand nine hundred pounds. A list of the sales and purchasers is given in Appendix I.

Arrangements were already under way for the despatch of several animals to their various destinations. The railway stations, Waverley and Princes Street, were expecting the arrival of numerous boxed and caged animals. Hannibal was sent off to Bristol by rail the same night. Of the others, some also went off that night, and some had already been taken away by their new owners. It took a day or two for them all to be cleared as the larger ones needed special crating and proper transport arrangements.

The auction the next day was, not surprisingly, a less spectacular affair. Up for auction were all the waggons, carriages, trappings, harness and all the other artefacts of the menagerie. Especially mentioned among the animal waggons and living vans were the big stage waggon and a "new" twelve-foot living van. The waggons fetched prices ranging from five to fifty pounds, with the exception of George's solid mahogany living van. George's van brought the highest price for any single item on the day – one hundred pounds. There were two sets of camel's shaft harness, a set of camel's tandem harness and the silver-plated elephant harness. Four sets of silver-mounted carriage harness, formerly the property of the Emperor of Austria, were sold at nine pounds ten shillings each. There were six canvas tilts 72 feet by 33 feet, "only been in use eight weeks" – Mr Fairgrieve was obviously keeping things in top-top condition until the very last moment. Then there were two large tubs for elephants, a wheeled shifting den, twelve railway lamps, numerous "oval glasses for night travelling, fitted in case", and a painting of a Mandrill's head by Horner. A supplementary catalogue contained lists of many smaller pieces and a list of over one hundred wood engravings, bills, posters and blocks whose value, when new, was estimated at a thousand pounds.

As a rounding off of the two-day sale, Mr Rice purchased from Mr Fairgrieve the goodwill of the menagerie. The total amount realised from the sale of the menagerie, including the horses, was between five and six thousand pounds.

So that was the end of Wombwell's Royal Number One Menagerie. But it was not the end of Wombwell's Menagerie. Mrs Edmonds, the niece of George Wombwell who owned Number Two, was rather concerned. All the newspaper publicity about the Edinburgh auction had given the impression that Wombwell's was no more. She may have been right to be concerned; it was bad for her business. Two days after it had printed its long report of the sale, 'The Times' felt obliged to print the following:

"In our account of the sale of a collection of wild animals at Edinburgh, which appeared in The Times of the 10th inst, it was described as "Wombwell's Menagerie". It would appear that this was not strictly correct. Upon the death of Mr Wombwell, in 1850, his menagerie, which was then in three parts, was specifically bequeathed to three distinct persons. Two of these parts have now been sold, but the third, which was given by him to his niece, Mrs Edmonds, is still in existence, and known as "Wombwell's Menagerie".

Quite true. The possibly false impression needed to be corrected. Mrs Edmonds had obviously given 'The Times' a piece of her mind. Now, of course, there was only one menagerie entitled to use the name 'Wombwell's' – hers. Being a show-business person, she did not fail to capitalise on 'The Times' publicity. The final sentence of the above piece was:

"We are informed by Mrs Edmonds that this (the Number Two) was the collection on which Mr Wombwell prided himself, and to which he always forwarded his most valuable purchases. It has existed for upwards of forty years."

George, nevertheless, had chosen to live with Number One, and was hardly likely to be content with the second best specimens from among his purchases. In any case, he had been dead for twenty-two years at the time of Mrs Edmonds' letter.

Three days later the same information was printed in the correspondence column of 'The Scotsman'. The letter was sent by Frank, Richardson & Sadler, presumably Mrs Edmonds' solicitors. The writers referred to "our client" rather than to Mrs Edmonds by name.

Scotland had always been the territory of the Number One menagerie. The following year, 1873, Bostock & Wombwell's Menagerie (an offshoot of the Number Two) went to Scotland. The menagerie had an African Elephant named Lizzie. Only she was able to pull the waggons out of the wet sands when they bogged down crossing an estuary where the tide was due to return, as they came back into the north west of England.

Mrs Edmonds' Number Two menagerie was indeed a major collection, already producing its own offshoots, destined to be passed to another generation, be asorbed into the Bostock & Wombwell network and carry on the Wombwell name.

Chapter 4

The Journey

"There have been", said the 'Edinburgh Daily Review' of the following Saturday, "several interesting little scenes at the railway station on the occasion of despatching to various parts of the country the wild animals recently sold at Wombwell's Menagerie".

James Jennison's total purchases for the Belle Vue Gardens in Manchester were Maharajah the elephant, Victoria the four-year-old pregnant Lioness, one Hamadryad Baboon and one Nilgau. They were booked onto the 10.05 express train from Waverley Station on Thursday 11th April, two days after their sale. Both Maharajah and Victoria created disturbances at the station. Victoria, however, remained safely enclosed in her crate.

It was normal practice for a few horse boxes to make up part of the train. One of these was reserved for the Elephant. Lorenzo accompanied Maharajah to the station and was to travel with him – whether or not in the horse box with the Elephant we do not know. That might have been dangerous but not outside the bounds of Lorenzo's character. Only eleven months before, a man named Paton was bringing an Elephant half Maharajah's age to London from Plymouth by rail. Paton travelled in the van with the elephant and was killed, although there were certain unanswered questions about the death, apart from the Elephant factor.

Maharajah was coaxed into the horse box and the doors were closed. There were probably a few smiles or grunts of satisfaction from the men concerned as the doors closed. A potentially difficult moment was over.

Then, Maharajah's head appeared through the front end of the waggon, not without the sound of splintering wood. For an Elephant accustomed to pushing loaded waggons into line, and moving loads that were too much for the horses, the wooden end of a horse box was no problem at all. He had simply pushed out the woodwork.

Railway officials gathered in alarm and Lorenzo watched. A raging elephant in the station was something the railway company had to take very seriously indeed. In any case, the express was due out in a matter of minutes. The chaotic scene of smashed woodwork, alarmed officials and fleeing passengers was intensified by the noise emitted by the elephant. His famous docility was abandoned, at least for the moment. One report described the noise as "an angry growl", another as "a loud snorting".

Before the officials had time to decide hastily upon a course of action between themselves and with Lorenzo, their words were drowned by a second explosion of timber being reduced to splinters. Maharajah had gone into reverse. The other end of the waggon was now open and the rear end of Maharajah was clearly visible.

A decision was reached remarkably quickly. What remained of the horse-box door was opened and Lorenzo got Maharajah out of the waggon and onto the platform. On the platform, and in Lorenzo's care, Maharajah was as docile and friendly as ever. Lorenzo said he would jolly well walk Maharajah to Manchester.

It is pure conjecture to suppose that Maharajah had acted on a signal from Lorenzo, Lorenzo who had probably made the Lion turn his back on the crowd at an invisible signal. It is no more than guesswork to think that Lorenzo was now out of a job and that travelling to Manchester on the train might be his last task. We do not know whether Jennison had offered him a job or not. What does seem clear is that the smashing of the waggon and the return to the platform were very well timed and co-ordinated. Maharajah was quite accustomed to the inside and the outside of waggons, admittedly not this particular one. Maybe this one did have a bad feel about it for Maharajah – maybe not. Certainly the publicity of the incident followed by the long walk would add to Lorenzo's fame, and so to his employment prospects if he really was out of a job. Lorenzo was a showman and he was also an animal keeper extraordinaire. The situation was totally in his control. We may be doing the man a grave injustice, or perhaps acknowledging his real superiority.

It is worth exploiting our hundred-year advantage and looking forward ten years to 1882, to the departure of Jumbo from London Zoo, bound for America. Jumbo's keeper was called Scott. Scott, in the great keeper tradition, was a taciturn and skilful man, who would not be moved in any direction until he was ready. (Scott was an extreme example; since he was the only one who could control Jumbo, he tended to treat the zoo administration with some contempt.) Jumbo refused to enter his crate in spite of tackle and chains. When it was decided to walk the elephant to the docks,

Jumbo set off willingly enough but would go no further than the zoo gates, and a touching don't-leave-me scene was acted between Scott and Jumbo, the latter kneeling in the road. The pantomime continued for some time, punctuated with several 'gestures' on Jumbo's part signifying his satisfaction with London and his reluctance to leave. Jumbo's purchaser was Barnum's. The Barnum representative soon cottoned on. He offered Scott a well-paid job with Jumbo. The elephant quite suddenly became co-operative and willing to leave. There would be not a single outward sign of collusion between Jumbo and Scott. Scott would simply appear to co-operate, as did Lorenzo at the station. We will never know if there really was a parallel; if Lorenzo was Scott's unwitting tutor. Either way both men had remarkable relationships with their animals.

The destroyed horse box was detached from the train and the 10.05 express for Manchester left ten minutes late.

The railway line between Waverley Station and Carlisle, via Hawick and Galashiels, was known as the Waverley line and was operated at the time by the North British Railway Company, later by the LNER. This was the way the express carried James Jennison's purchases to Manchester. The last train to run on this line, on 6th January 1969, was not without incident, either. David Steel was on the train and he had to get out and use all his persuasive powers to disperse the people blocking the line in protest at its closure. The other route south to Manchester from Edinburgh was the London & North Western (later LMS) route from Princes Street, via Symington and Beattock. This was the line to survive.

With remarkably little delay, Lorenzo chose to walk the North British route of the 10.05 express. That same day he and Maharajah set off. They covered about twenty miles and spent the night at Stow.

The newspapers (the lesser ones copying the greater ones) claimed that Maharajah could cover thirty to forty miles in a day, and so predicted that the pair would reach Manchester in about a week. That may have been possible but one or both of the pair chose a slower pace and their daily average was just over twenty.

The second day's walk was from Stow to Hawick, a distance of about twenty-six miles. This second stage of the Journey was still reported by the Edinburgh press ('The Daily Review'). For the occasion of the report Majarajah was called Big Ben, which might have been mere journalese or might suggest that the name of Maharajah was bestowed on him later. The pair arrived at Hawick about six o'clock on Friday evening and the elephant seemed not at all disturbed by the large crowd of youngsters who followed him along the street. In fact, the paper reported that he was 'greatly pleased with his numerous escort''. The pair stayed at the Bridge Hotel, which does not seem to be there any more, certainly anywhere near the bridge.

Many of the inns of the day had the familiar arch, big enough for stage coaches, which led to the coach yard and stables. Maharajah would be able to get through the arch in most cases. If there was a stable big enough, Maharajah (and Lorenzo?) would spend the night there. Otherwise the elephant would simply spend the night in the stable yard, as was the case at the Bridge Hotel, Hawick.

As we have seen, elephants walking the highways were not uncommon. One does not have to dig too deep to find their tracks. In one area of north Lancashire, for example, the libraries will produce photographs of unnamed elephants in the streets of Bowness and Sedbergh. It was only slightly less unusual for the elephant to stay at an inn. During this very month of April 1872 Lizzie, the African Elephant with Mrs Edmonds' establishment, was staying at an inn in Staffordshire where the youngsters were less than kind to her, as we shall see. It would be more unusual for one elephant and one man to arrive at the inn seeking accommodation. The innkeepers' open mindedness might have been tested from time to time. A shadow of their incredulity still remained when I visited one of the inns, a hundred and fifteen years later, and suggested to the bartender that an elephant had stayed there.

Business at the Bridge Hotel was good that night. The people of the town turned out to admire the animal and the Hawick Express not only described Maharajah as "one of the best specimens" but got Mr Jennison's name correct in the report. He had been referred to as Mr Jennings and Mr Jamieson by different papers. One paper reporting the Edinburgh sale even claimed that Maharajah had been bought by Mr Rice. Well, at least they were not copying from the other papers. The Hawick Express did not give the elephant a name.

The reporter who had referred to the elephant as Big Ben clearly had literary ambitions. In forecasting the next stage of the journey – from Hawick to Langholm – he used the rather striking phrase, "via the ancient desolation of Mosspaul''. It is a vague phrase but the general idea is clear enough. The landscape of the stretch between Hawick and Langholm has changed much less than the stages, say, south of Preston. The area does indeed have a feeling of remoteness in its hilly beauty. The fact that once the Waverley line cut through it, and does so no longer, is made up for by the presence of a metalled road. An aspect of end-of-century travel, sometimes overlooked and overshadowed by our total acceptance of tarmacadam, was the cloud of dust which accompanied every road traveller in dry weather, making a bath a necessity and rendering the travellers visible for some miles distant.

To my mind, though, the most scenically dramatic stretch of the whole journey would be over Shap, between Penrith and Kendal. It is reasonable to suppose that the Scottish local reporter had never visited Shap, and anyway Lorenzo and Maharajah had not got there yet.

The third day brought the pair over the border into England, and to Carlisle. The extant Carlisle papers do not record their passage through the town, although other papers may have done so. We do know from other sources that they came that way and it is exactly the right distance from Langholm for them to have stayed the night there. The pair were following what we now call the A6, having followed the A7 south from Edinburgh. From Carlisle the route had to take them through yet more spectacular scenery to Penrith and then, for the sixth night of the journey, to Kendal. In Kendal they spent the night at the White Hart Inn which still stands, complete with coach arch and stable-yard area, on the main street of the town. They set off early next morning, Lorenzo in front and Maharajah "jogging along at a good pace behind his keeper" in the words of the Kendal Mercury. Perhaps Lorenzo liked to get quickly out of towns before allowing their travel to assume its more enjoyable pace.

On Wednesday, 17th April, they stayed at the Commercial Hotel in Lancaster and resumed their journey the next morning as usual. The local paper was accurate in reporting the daily average as about twenty miles since they had left Edinburgh.

From this point onwards the route would become more and more unrecognisable if its present scenery were viewed with Lorenzo's nineteenth-century eyes. With Lancashire still at the peak of its industrial power, the elephant and its keeper, while causing a series of local stirs, might be regarded as less newsworthy in the hurly burly of the textile towns. The Preston newspapers, at least those currently available in the Preston Central Library, did not seem to find Maharajah interesting enough to record his passage, but, again, we know the pair came that way and its distance was, again, exactly right for an overnight stay.

Just north west of Manchester Lorenzo and Maharajah left the A6 route and veered towards Bolton. They followed the present A673 towards the town. It is a wide road but still has several relatively unspoilt stretches where the scenery may be not totally unlike that seen by the pair as the neared their destination. The Bolton Evening News, still a thriving paper at the time of writing, noted their presence in the town and mentioned an "eight day" journey.

The distance from Bolton to Manchester is less than twenty miles. This shorter journey on the final stage would allow them to arrive at Belle Vue during the afternoon of a busy Saturday and so permit Belle Vue to stage a welcome.

The front page of the 'Manchester Guardian' was, as was the custom at the time, devoted to paid advertisements in columns – a practice which 'The Times' continued much longer than its imitators. Belle Vue used the front page regularly, sometimes several times a week, and sometimes buying several column inches to publicise a special firework tableau or other outstanding event.

On Saturday 20th April, in addition to its other, regular advertisements, the Manchester Guardian carried this one, which named Maharajah:

> The Fine Male Indian Elephant, Maharajah, purchased at the sale of Wombwell's Menagerie, at Edinburgh, will ARRIVE at the Gardens THIS DAY at about 2 p.m., having travelled by road from Scotland, via Carlisle, Kendal, Lancaster, Preston and Bolton, to Manchester.

They had been walking for ten days.

Chapter 5

The Disputed Toll

I have indicated already that an elephant walking along the roads of Britain was a cause for curiosity and local excitement, but not national coverage. Maharajah's walk generated more than the usual excitement partly because it arose out of the Edinburgh sale, which **was** national news, partly because of the smashed van incident and partly because Edinburgh – Manchester was rather a long hop.

It was not long after the event that the walk began to turn into a kind of legend or animal fable, and it began to acquire those apocryphal details which become harder and harder to unravel as time goes by.

Two of these details can be dealt with fairly easily as they are clearly not true. Both of them are mentioned by C H Keeling in his book about Belle Vue. The first is that the walk was attributed not to Maharajah but to another elephant called Sally. Sally was a female Asiatic Elephant already at Belle Vue when Maharajah arrived. The fact that the two elephants spent some years together at Belle Vue is the probable cause of their confusion. The second is that the walk was not done by an elephant at all, but by a rhinoceros. This unlikely tale was discovered by Mr Keeling in an old children's book called The Splendid Book of Animals. While both of these variations are very dismissable as far as facts are concerned, they demonstrate very well how the walk had entered the realms of folklore.

A third legend about Maharajah merits more investigation. This legend was refuted – totally squashed, in fact – by The Manchester Guardian only three weeks after Maharajah's arrival in Manchester, and yet it persisted, and within a year or two had involved at least one famous painter and the Royal Academy, and was still being retold as fact well into the twentieth century.

The legend, allowing for variations, was this. On their journey Lorenzo and Maharajah undoubtedly passed through a few toll gates. On one such occasion a dispute arose between the gate keeper and Lorenzo about how much it cost for an elephant to pass through. The dispute grew heated and was solved only when

Maharajah either lifted the gate off its hinges or simply smashed it down with his head. Either way, Lorenzo and Maharajah proceeded peacefully on their way, leaving a furious toll-gate keeper behind them.

Let us first accept the fact that almost all those who have ever had to stop and pay at a toll gate have wished that they had an elephant (or, today, a tank) with them that could disregard the gate. Maharajah was a perfect candidate for this dream of wish fulfilment. Not only was he passing through several toll gates, but he had already and actually smashed up a railway waggon. What is more, twenty-seven years later, Lorenzo was to tell a reporter how Maharajah had removed the door posts of an inn stable in Scotland, while passing through the narrow doorway.

Then we must seriously consider the possibility that one of those nineteenth-century peripatetic elephants, sometime and somewhere, had really demolished a toll gate and continued its journey unabashed. There is some evidence for this, too.

Out of this fusion of railway van, stable door, existing legend and wish fulfilment grew the indisputable new fact that by the end of the walk people were associating Maharajah with demolished toll gates.

The newspapers of the time took the trouble to note that Maharajah walked from here to there, and stayed at this inn and that hotel. Nowhere in those reports is there a mention of a toll-gate incident, except – and this is the fascinating part – The Manchester Guardian of 11th May which denied the whole thing in these words:

> "He was not put to the necessity told in a story of one elephant of lifting a toll gate off its hinges; for all gates were open to him free, inasmuch as the gate keepers could not rate him as horse, cow, ass or sheep, for which alone they had legal authority to charge."

This gem of a snippet tells us two things: one, that the elephant and toll-gate story already existed; two, that the story was associated with Maharajah (by its very denial) three weeks after the walk.

Enter now Heywood Hardy, established artist in oils and water colours, aged twenty-nine in 1872. Many people are familiar with Heywood Hardy's style without ever having heard his name. He painted people on horseback. He painted hunting scenes, local squires, dashing young men and pretty maidens both rustic and gentle. His horses are well bred and well kept, but they are always realistic. Viewed with twentieth-century eyes Heywood Hardy is the archetypal chocolate-box and birthday-card painter. He was a genre painter and his characters sometimes wore the clothes of an age recently passed. He did, however, have a taste for the zoological and for the occasional exotic beast. His works included a zoo sketch called 'Just Before Feeding Time' and an 'Elephant Head' sketch, both dated in the 1870s. Even more noteworthy was a painting which he exhibited at the Royal Academy in 1875 called 'The Disputed Toll'. This painting is almost certainly the one showing two men discussing something at a toll gate. One man is the gate keeper, the other man has an elephant. The elephant has not yet passed through the gate. The subject was perfect for him. Hardy was a painter of animals and he was also a painter of ever so slightly romanticized moments from the past.

The painting changed hands several times as paintings do. At one point between the world wars it fetched a price of six hundred guineas. In 1952 it was given as a present to Gerald Iles, Zoological Director of Belle Vue. The story of how Iles acquired the painting is told in his own book, 'At Home in the Zoo'. Iles was interested in the painting because it showed a Belle Vue elephant at its most famous moment. Iles claims that Heywood Hardy visited Belle Vue to talk with Lorenzo and make sketches of Maharajah. Heywood Hardy was very much a southerner and there would certainly be elephants more accessible to him than one in Manchester, but there is no reason to believe that he did not venture north to visit Belle Vue. Was Hardy just viewing Maharajah as the most suitable model for his painting or did he want to paint Maharajah because he believed that here was the actual gate smasher? His journey to Belle Vue suggests the latter.

Gerald Iles relates how, after the publicity of his receiving 'The Disputed Toll' as a gift, another Manchester person contacted him to say that he, too, had a picture called 'The Disputed Toll'. This was a much smaller one but showed basically the same scene and could have been a preparatory work. It is interesting that this second picture was also in Manchester.

Gerald Iles left Belle Vue in 1957 and took 'The Disputed Toll' with him to Canada where, presumably, it still is. I have never seen it but I believe I have seen the smaller one. Maharajah's skeleton is on public view in Manchester Museum. Displayed with the skeleton is a small painting called 'The Disputed Toll'. The museum sign explains that the skeleton is that of the famous Belle Vue elephant who walked from Edinburgh to Manchester and who smashed a toll gate on the way, and here is a picture which celebrates the incident. Quite fair; that is the accepted story. The figures in the painting, what is more, wear slightly old-fashioned clothes; old-fashioned, that is, for 1872. A representative Heywood Hardy. The picture is unsigned and has recently been for conservation treatment. The museum has no record of how it acquired the picture. (The museum authorities were most helpful, I must add, in allowing me to search through old correspondence and record books.) I am assuming that the small picture on view at Manchester museum is the small one mentioned by Gerald Iles, which has since been donated to the museum. Unless, of course, there are three Disputed Tolls.

On close inspection, the elephant in the Manchester museum picture has a bar across his tusks. Let us briefly digress and discuss Maharajah's bar.

Although we do not know exactly when the bar became attached to Maharajah's tusks, it was certainly there during some of his Belle Vue years. In spite of the elephant's fame, no-one ever seemed to refer to it when writing about him during his lifetime. Until recently, the displayed information at Manchester Museum, as supplied by keeper Stansfield, a young contemporary of Lorenzo, stated that it was fixed at Belle Vue after Maharajah's arrival. I am inclined to agree with this but any kind of verification seems to be lacking.

There is as much mystery surrounding the removal of the bar as there is about its fixing. Gerald Iles heard the unlikely story that Maharajah had bled to death when the tusk ends (and bar) were sawn off. Iles rightly dismissed the story; first, because tusks do not bleed, and secondly because both sides of the saw cuts still existed and Iles argued that the tusks themselves had become a little rounded with wear, showing that the elephant had lived for some time after the ends had been sawn off. Iles himself kept the tusk ends attached to the bar. The tusks (attached to the skeleton) were first in the Belle Vue museum and later in the Manchester museum.

It is, of course, true that tusks do not bleed, but the story was probably not pure fantasy. George Jennison tells how Maharajah was once walking across a wooden bridge over the lake. One of the planks broke beneath Maharajah's weight. The elephant fell and splintered a tusk so badly that it had to be sawn off "with great loss of blood". This could well be the occasion which caused the bar to be finally removed. But what was the origin of the blood in the story? If Maharajah had a bad fall, as opposed to a more straightforward operation removing the bar, and a tusk was so badly splintered that it had to be removed, then that tusk would very likely be severely dislodged within its socket, and blood may well have flowed freely. If one examines the sawn ends of the tusks attached to Maharajah's skeleton in the Manchester museum, one will see that the left tusk is indeed cleanly sawn, in spite of subsequent wear and tear. The right tusk, however, has a much more 'broken' look about it and there is a cavity in the end of it which seems to have been filled or repaired either by nature or by man. This might suggest that it was the right tusk which was damaged on the bridge that day. The tusk points, still attached to the bar, went to Canada with Gerald Iles and 'The Disputed Toll'. The actual year of the accident has not revealed itself but George Jennison (only a small child when Maharajah was alive) states that Maharajah lived for some time after the accident "but was never the same animal afterwards".

There seems to be little evidence to support the simple and common belief that the tusks were shortened because Maharajah lost his famed docility, and was potentially dangerous – although that is always possible. If I were an elephant with a bar fixed permanently across my tusks I believe I would frequently appear to be violent – if only because of my attempts to get the bar off, using any convenient wall, tree, etc, which might be damaged in the process. But that is more conjecture.

If we are to take Hardy's painting as a real representation, then the bar was a Wombwell's fixture and not a Belle Vue fixture. Hardy (the presumed author of the smaller painting) clearly worked on the assumption that it had been fixed before the journey. While there had been plenty of time for Belle Vue to fix it before Hardy's visit, and no mention of it at all when Maharajah was a Wombwell's elephant, both of these possibilities rest solely on circumstantial evidence. By including the bar in the picture, the painter of the small picture was portraying the real Maharajah as the elephant of the toll gate. By 1874, or thereabouts, when Hardy was doing the painting, the identity of Maharajah and the toll gate seem to have become inseparable.

If the situation is clear so far, it is about to be fogged again. A book called 'Life at the Zoo' by a perceptive writer called Charles Cornish, published in 1896, has a chapter about elephants in it. That chapter contains these words:

> "The clever picture of the 'Disputed Toll' by Charlton
> Adams, in which an elephant is painted breaking open a
> turnpike gate, records an amusing incident of elephant
> travel which occurred many years ago outside the pretty
> little town of Sidmouth in South Devon. Van Amburgh's
> show was expected, and the turnpike keeper locked the

gate and demanded toll, not only for the cars but for the animals. The elephant was leading the way, and after much fruitless argument, its keeper, slipping through the turnstile for foot passengers, said to the elephant, "Come along, Fido", and the animal at once lifted the gate off its hinges and walked through."

Van Ambergh's? Sidmouth? Charlton Adams? Fido? Fido, indeed!

Cornish several times refers to paintings in his book, and seems to know a little about art. Apart from the other differences, could he really be mistaking Heywood Hardy for Charlton Adams? And who is Charlton Adams, anyway? There were one or two painters called Adams who did animals but no-one called Charlton seems to have been recorded. The closest name seems to be Charles J Adams but there is no further connection. We can disregard 'Fido' as an imaginary name but Cornish would be unlikely to invent an artist. What is more, in the Manchester Museum picture, Maharajah is not "breaking open a turnpike gate". He may be about to, but he has not yet started. We seem to be talking about a different picture.

Until someone produces some more evidence, I posit the following hypothesis.

The disputed toll was probably a real incident – possibly the Sidmouth one. It turned from an incident into a theme. It was interpreted by more than one painter and was part of the oral tradition among travelling and zoo people. It was a suitable subject for Heywood Hardy. The theme became attached to Maharajah, in particular, after he had achieved fame as a carriage smasher and long-distance walker. Hardy believed Maharajah to be the actual perpetrator of the act and decided to paint his own interpretation of the Toll theme. Hardy's painting was a good one and gained recognition in its own right. It became the definitive one, perhaps by being hung at the Royal Academy. Other versions were overlooked, lost or forgotten. Maharajah, because he was in the painting, had already smashed a railway carriage and was famous anyway, became totally established as the one and only 'Toll Gate' elephant.

One might ask why Lorenzo simply did not tell Hardy that Maharajah had never interfered with a toll gate. There are several reasonable answers. It would not, I suggest, be compatible with Lorenzo's character to enlighten the gentleman who had travelled from London to do a painting of an incident believed by the gentleman to be true. Neither would it be to Lorenzo's advantage; not only would he be disappointing the artist, but he would be seriously detracting from the fame of his own career. Lorenzo would have been foolish to turn down the opportunity of having his elephant painted and exhibited by a recognised artist. In any case, Hardy's painting was not of an elephant damaging a toll gate; it was of one man with an elephant, discussing something with another man by a toll gate. Both Lorenzo and Hardy could depend on the painting's title, the public imagination and existing rumours to supply any further details. Both their careers depended, to a degree, on an imaginative response to their work by the public. There is also the theoretical possibility of collusion between keeper and painter to produce a picture which could not be disputed.

C.V.A. Peel told the Maharajah–Toll Gate story as true in his 1903 book. Geoffrey Schomberg did likewise in 1957, and so did Gerald Iles in 1960. We do not know their sources, although each writer had very probably read his predecessor's book. It is a good story and worth repeating, but its real source does not seem to be in the walk of Maharajah from Edinburgh to Manchester.

Let us look back to a mere three weeks after the walk. The Manchester Guardian said that Maharajah had not done anything of the kind. That is still a strange piece of news.

Chapter 6

Lizzie

The story in this short chapter is only incidental to the story of Maharajah. The events took place in the same week that Maharajah spent walking from Edinburgh. The story touches upon the Edinburgh auction and concerns a Wombwell menagerie and a Wombwell elephant who led a life not at all unlike that led by Maharajah until he was sold to James Jennison. It is also about a menagerie elephant staying at an inn and the contact of that elephant with some human behaviour.

A man named James Bostock had joined the Number Two Menagerie in 1839 as waggoner and horse keeper. He married the sister of Mrs Edmonds the proprietor and so joined the Wombwell family. James and his wife formed their own menagerie, Bostock & Wombwell's, and their sons were eventually to absorb the Number Two and so continue and develop the Wombwell traditions. We have seen that the Number Three came to an end shortly after George's death, and the Number One at the Edinburgh auction. Number Two, as an independent menagerie, lasted until 1889 when Mrs Edmonds sold the titles and some of the animals to E. H. Bostock, one of James's sons. The remaining animals were disposed of at a sale in Liverpool. But that was in the future. While Maharajah was walking to Manchester, the Number Two and Bostock & Wombwell's were separate menageries.

Three of the camels bought by Mr Bostock at the Edinburgh auction had met up with Bostock & Wombwell's Menagerie in Staffordshire. The camels and the Bostock & Wombwell African Elephant, Lizzie, found themselves at the Angel Inn, Hanley.

The animals were in the stable yard of the inn. The usual crowd of curious onlookers, including some boys, was gathered in the yard. The boys were feeding some nuts to Lizzie. Lizzie, like Maharajah and many other menagerie elephants, was practised and skilled at searching out food from the public. (Maharajah was not the only elephant reputed to take food for himself and coins for his keeper.) As the nuts ran out, the boys offered stones to Lizzie. Needless to say, she was not interested. The stones, instead of being offered to her, were then thrown at her. Witnesses later confirmed that at least one stone was thrown at her.

In addition to the crowd of boys, the ostler, the inn keeper named Jones and the Wombwell's keeper were also in the yard when Lizzie picked up one of the boys in her trunk. The name of the boy was George Stanton. The keeper was (according to witnesses speaking later) about five or six yards away. He later insisted that he was only two yards away. The facts were that he was there, there was a small crowd, and that someone was throwing stones at the elephant. The keeper did not see Lizzie actually pick Stanton up.

The keeper (another good one?) shouted at the elephant and the elephant released Stanton. Jones, the inn keeper, was walking away at the time and turned round only to see Lissie drop the boy. The ostler later said he saw the elephant pick up Stanton with her trunk and throw him against a wall, where she held him until her keeper called. (Is this possible?)

The form of the 'attack' (defence?) was never known in detail. There was a mass of conflicting evidence.

George Stanton was taken to hospital and died there from wounds in the head and severe internal injuries. He died on the Saturday or Sunday night (reports differ) of the weekend of April 14th, while Maharajah was passing through Langholm.

The inquest was on Wednesday the 17th. The coroner remarked on the conflicting nature of the evidence but had no doubt that the boys had teased Lizzie. The foreman of the jury had hard words to say about the keeper, who seemed to have been half a dozen yards away while there was a crowd round the elephant. The jury returned an open verdict that the boy died from the effects of being crushed by an elephant.

There have been horrific incidents where human beings have actually brought an elephant to 'justice' after a comparable incident. Fortunately this was not the case in Staffordshire in 1872. Lizzie lived until 1888. She died at work in Llansawell in South Wales. The moving of her dead body presented no small problem. Her outer form was preserved, and can still be seen, at the museum in Swansea. She was one of at least three Wombwell's elephants preserved in city museums. There was Roger (also Bostock & Wombwell's) in Glasgow, and the skeleton of Maharajah in Manchester.

Chapter 7

The Belle Vue Years

In the 1890s C. J. Cornish estimated that there were one hundred and thirteen elephants in Europe.

> "Russia owns eighteen, Sweden and Norway four, France and Belgium ten each, seven of which are in the great travelling menagerie of the Lockharts, which migrates across the Franco-Belgian frontier; Germany has thirty-four, and England about the same number; Holland has eight, and Italy two."

The British elephants were supplied almost entirely from Burma. Elephants arrived in Europe when they were quite young and were not difficult to obtain.

> "Anyone who pleases (wrote Cornish) may become the owner of a sober, well-behaved little elephant from four to five feet high, delivered at the docks for from £105 to £120, or not more than the average price paid for a first-class shire horse."

The majority of British elephants belonged to the larger circuses and menageries where they tended to lead quite active lives. The few major zoos at the time were, quite naturally, proud of their own elephants which led an existence only slightly more leisurely than their counterparts in the menageries. It is interesting to note, as an aside, that the 'leisurely' life of many of the higher mammals in modern zoological gardens has been the subject of much research, which has tended to show that the animals thrive on a full routine, with plenty of contact and tasks to perform.

There were, and nearly always have been, fewer African than Asiatic Elephants in Europe. One reason for their scarcity at the end of the nineteenth century was the blockade of the traditional trade route out of Africa, at Khartoum, caused by the religious wars which involved General Gordon. At the time that Cornish was writing, a few years after Maharajah's death but while Sally was still giving daily rides at Belle Vue, there were only seven African Elephants in Europe, of which three were in Britain. One was at

London Zoo, one was at Belle Vue and the third, of whom we have already heard, was Lizzie with Bostock & Wombwell's. The idea that Asiatic Elephants were easier to train, and were more tractable generally, was well established in the animal world. It was African Elephants, however, who had first been seen in Europe, via the Romans, and there are several instances of amazingly cool and intelligent behaviour by British African Elephants. Lizzie, for example, had been involved in a tent fire during which her back had been severely burnt by blazing flare fuel. Only the audience had panicked.

The African Elephant at London was arguably the most famous elephant in recorded history; Maharajah's contemporary, Jumbo. Jumbo was only four feet high when he arrived in London from the Jardin des Plantes in exchange for an Asian rhinoceros, but grew to over eleven feet in his sixteen-year stay, and even then was probably not fully grown. Scott, Jumbo's keeper, was the only man who could control him. Scott realised how indispensible he was to the zoo and became something of an eccentric autocrat. He resisted all attempts to provide him with an assistant, as attempts to dilute his power. We have already noted his probable role in the matter of Jumbo's departure for the docks. If Scott was indispensible to London, Jumbo was, of course, indispensible to Scott. The pair sailed for America on the 'Assyrian Monarch' on 25th March 1883.

After Jumbo's death in Canada, Scott declined a well-paid job with Barnum's (because he would have to wear an exotic costume, so the story goes) and remained as a keeper to the body of Jumbo which had been preserved by a taxidermist. The job was more necessary than it might appear; souvenir hunters would soon have reduced the body to nothing.

Scott was clearly an animal keeper of exceptional ability and undoubted devotion to Jumbo. One has the distinct impression that he never really found himself again once Jumbo was dead. Lorenzo and Maharajah almost certainly had a comparable relationship. Lorenzo's world-view was perhaps a little wider than Scott's, and his character a little stronger. The Belle Vue elephants were lucky enough to have Lorenzo's care for forty years, only ten of which Lorenzo shared with Maharajah.

Belle Vue's first elephant, from Ceylon, had arrived there around 1860 and lived there maybe seven years. This elephant lived in the ground-floor Menagerie underneath the museum. She seems to have been replaced by Sally, the Asiatic Elephant who arrived in 1869 as a small young animal. Because of her small size Sally quickly became a pet of the staff and spent much of the daytime in the kitchen with them. She was put in a stable at night. On one occasion when she was alarmed during the night she crashed through two doors out of the stable and made for the kitchen where she felt secure. Maharajah joined her in 1872 and the pair became a team and well known in a variety of public events. Maharajah and Sally were sentimentally seen as 'a couple' in the public mind, in the same way that Jumbo and Alice were in London. Maharajah saw much more of Sally than Jumbo ever saw of Alice.

The site of Belle Vue is now in the inner ring of Manchester's urban sprawl. The Gorton-Longsight area is not the dream of the socially aspirant. In 1872, however, it was still out of the city. Belle Vue was widely known throughout Britain and was a household name in Manchester. Special Belle Vue excursion trains ran from other towns, often well outside the area. It had its own railway station. There were other pleasure gardens and botanical gardens in the Manchester area but Belle Vue's zoological collection was unique in the North of England. The zoo was what gave Belle Vue its particular character. While the range of its attractions was wide and impressive (a sports stadium, a lake with boats, museum, restaurants, grottoes and a host of other things) the zoological collection was anything but an appendage to the other entertainments. The animals were taken very seriously by the owners and the staff. The fact that James Jennison was prepared to travel to Edinburgh and buy just four animals, one of which cost £680, was evidence enough of the animals' prestige. Not until a hundred years later did the 1970s management consider the zoological collection to be a burden. The animals were then dispersed and Belle Vue immediately lost its heart and its identity; and in the closure an Elephant lost its life. Other animals had been shot in preparation. Once the zoo was gone, the other attractions began to disappear one by one.

The Belle Vue Gardens were approaching forty years of age when Maharajah approached them from Bolton. John Jennison had been the founder and the whole Belle Vue complex was operated by the Jennison family until 1928. The family provided Belle Vue with a series of imaginative directors and Manchester with some distinguished citizens.

The animals, as we have seen, were at the heart of the matter, but the events which caused more holding of breath, occupied most newspaper advertising and attracted more publicity of the adulatory kind were the firework displays. They were displays of their kind which have possibly not been surpassed. Like theatrical performances they had a theme and a title, and the same show was put on each night throughout the season. Each year had a new theme and title. Each new show, heralded by much publicity, had its premiere at the Whit holiday. Whit was a major urban festival in Manchester. It has now been exchanged, nationally, for the incredibly dull non-event called Spring Bank Holiday.

The firework shows were usually mounted by a London firm called Danson, which was held in some reverence by Manchester people. The show in the year of Maharajah's arrival was:

"Napoleon Crossing the Alps by the Pass of Mont St Bernard, in June 1800"

Belle Vue's publicity for this show, on the front pages of the Manchester Guardian could almost be measured in column feet rather than column inches (closely-packed words, not sensational big lettering). The final paragraph of the piece read:

"Admission: Before 4 o'clock 6d, after that hour 1s. The Celebrated Performing Elephant, Maharajah, recently purchased, along with his keeper, will appear daily, and many other important additions have been made to the Zoological Collection."

That appeared on 11th May, about three weeks after Maharajah's arrival. For that same season a new stable, for one hundred and fifty visitors' horses and their traps or carriages, had been erected. It measured one hundred yards by twelve.

A long publicity article in the same paper the following week mentioned the lioness recently bought from Wombwell's, and devoted two hundred words to Maharajah. It was this article which contained those words about the elephant **not** lifting a toll gate off its hinges.

There are signs that Lorenzo the Lion Tamer of Wombwell's was to acquire, during his Belle Vue years, the almost classic temperament of great animal keepers; laconic, taciturn and seeming to prefer the company of his charges to most humans.

Meanwhile, another ex-Wombwell's keeper at Belle Vue, Thomas Davy, was having a spot of trouble. Thomas, like many keepers, was known as a quiet, God-fearing man. A lioness escaped in 1874. She had jumped through a window and had frightened only a cat and a watchman. She had cubs and might have been in a sensitive mood. Davy found the lioness lying near the Jennisons' private offices about fifty yards from her den. The keeper picked up two of her cubs and walked towards the lioness, speaking softly to her. The lioness sniffed at her cubs, got up and followed Davy back to her den. Like Lorenzo, Thomas Davy did not only seem fearless in his serene approach to animals, but was also somewhat non-conformist in his work. He took his dogs for walks like any other dog owner, but returned them to the lion cage, their home, afterwards. The only precaution he took was to remove them when the lions were feeding.

An entertaining contemporary account of Belle Vue during the Maharajah period appeared in 'The City Jackdaw', a weekly "humorous and satirical journal" (one penny), now defunct. The account purports to tell the story of one family's visit there, and the writer uses the pseudonym "Paterfamilias". First, though, the writer takes a sideswipe at those clergy who had denounced Belle Vue from the pulpit. He refers to them as "those who are fond of denouncing as sour and unwholesome grapes which they have not tasted".

". . . these gardens", he maintains, "are a wholesome, instructive and entertaining resort. We leave, it is true, before night has fallen, because youngsters' bedtime has come . . . but I see no harm in holding out the prospect to my eldest boy and girl that in a year or two, if they are good, they will be allowed to remain with me to see the fireworks.

Setting out after an early dinner, and selecting a Tuesday, Thursday or Friday, when the gardens are quietest, we reach the ground about three, heavily laden with satchels and packages containing our sandwiches, cake, tea and other mysteries. Directly we are inside the grounds there is a general burst from our care, and the boys, like hounds unleashed, are scampering off amongst the macaws, parroquets and cockatoos, pretending to renew old acquaintance. The picture has its share of admiration before we diverge to the right, where, if the steam velocipedes are going, the entire family are soon mounted, and whooping and hallooing as they chase each other round the mimic circus. If the 'Little Britain' has got up steam we make one circuit of the lake, under license of the Board of Trade, before trans-shipping into one of those capacious, unupsettable, flat-bottomed boats or barges, which are let out to visitors by the hour. Having the lake practically to ourselves we steer a clear course, disturbing the wild fowl near the island, and flushing a brace of rather shame-faced lovers near the Gorton end, cooing together on one of those

'Seats beneath the shade
For talking age and whispering lovers made'

which Messrs Jennison have considerately placed in these retired nooks. Cooling the enthusiasms of the youngsters with a few penny ices, we scamper across the Italian gardens to the bear pits, where sundry attempts to bribe the white bears into their pond, and the brown ones to the top of their ladder, are made amid great glee – the former successful, the latter an ignominious failure. Passing over the lawn at the back of the picture we reach the ponds dedicated to waterfowl, and a special tank in which we have the good luck to see the seals feeding. We are tempted into the maze, but the site of the long necks of two giraffes grazing in the paddock is too much for us, and we are attracted towards them. These graceful animals – the type of haughty aristocrats with small heads and very little in them, combined with an uncommon assumption of dignity – afford us much amusement and the foundation for sundry jokes, which, at any rate, make the children laugh. The youngsters are fresh enough even to appreciate that old saying concerning the difficulty of dealing with a yard of sore throat. We enjoy ourselves among the zoological collection, and afterwards in the gardens, and especially at the beaver-pond – a department of Messrs Jennisons' enterprise which is every year extending. But before we settle down to tea, let us step for half an hour into the Museum. We suspect the proportion of visitors to the gardens who even enter the Museum is very small, and yet it is one of the most interesting sights within the grounds. To begin with, the serpent boxes are a real wonder. There they lie folded up in immense coils, some of them nearly as thick as a blacksmith's arm, but stingless, and unless they can get a chance of a bite, quite harmless. An obliging attendant lifted out two or three of the smaller specimens, which very soon began to disperse with a gliding motion over the floor, costing no little trouble in their recovery. The museum comprises two long galleries, each lined on either side with glass cases, in which are exhibited the stuffed forms of animals which have closed their public career in the gardens. If the attendant is in a chatty humour, you may learn from him strange tales as to their history.

But the tea! That is the crowning event of the day. Materfamilias has brought ample supplies of her best Bohea, and hot water is to be had in the room set apart for private picnic parties, such as ours, at a nominal charge. With our own snowy table cloth spread, and covered with dishes (of which any supply can be had at the counter), we fall to with zest; and after reviving ourselves we set out to renew our evening pleasure. How the children got on the back of Maharajah, with the Old Fogie acting as Mahout, and how the Editor went spooning in the maze with Aunt Jane . . . ''

In this, as in several other contemporary pieces, Maharajah is the only animal individually identified and named.

The Museum referred to in the piece was on the upper floor of a building just inside the entrance, and reached by a spiral staircase from the ground floor. The ground floor was called The Menagerie and housed, predictably, a mixed collection of animals, mainly small ones, and possibly Sally the elephant. The building had certainly been Sally's home when she was small but she could have been too big for it by Maharajah's time. With the arrival of Maharajah a new glass-roofed house for the elephants was erected near the firework lake. It served the elephants for a year or two and continued as a refreshment room after the elephants had had their own brick building erected.

Maharajah and Sally gave rides to thousands of children, usually with Lorenzo supervising. A postcard of elephant rides at Belle Vue, circa 1905, shows a painting of what is possibly Maharajah, and a bearded gentleman in uniform, looking remarkably like Lorenzo. The elephants had other jobs, too. Maharajah was not only the chief actor in the central incident of 'The Prince of Calcutta', the firework spectacle of 1876, but gave a fine performance, according to reviews. George Jennison, a generation later, recalled how, as a child of four and a half, he was taken to the show by a keeper. He wore the keeper's hat and was told to hold tight when the elephant knelt down for the prince to descend. 'The City Jackdaw' described the same scene.

"A giant balloon emerges from the gloom, and ascends like a pale ghost to mid-air, where, at an immense height, it is consumed in flames. The fountains of coloured fire send their many-hued globules into the air, like a thousand Chinese jugglers tossing myriads of balls in unceasing play. Meanwhile, the picture is getting lit up, and the streets are filled with moving masses. Regiments of soldiers, British and native, parade the street to festive music – Rajahs, in all the brilliance and gorgeous attire and peacocks' feathers, troop along in picturesque disorder, mounted on elephants, real and sham – the latter so cleverly constructed as to puzzle the uninstructed observer which is the genuine article and which the imitation. Last of all enters the Prince of Wales mounted on the huge but docile Maharajah".

And this was just one scene. That adjective 'docile' was still being applied to Maharajah.

Sally and Maharajah regularly paraded in the city-wide Whit Walks – parades over two days participated in by virtually every member of every church in the city. The elephants were also the recognised leaders in the May Day processions when their loads were hams from Broady's in Shudehill. George Jennison recalls riding on top of the load on the return journey clutching a shining sixpence from Mr Broady.

Sally was a timid but not troublesome elephant. Animals in Lorenzo's care were possibly never too troublesome. After Maharajah's time, Sally did on one occasion have a quarrel with Dinah, another female Asiatic. Sally charged Dinah and knocked her over. Dinah fell on a solid iron bench which "looked like a concertina" after the incident, according to George Jennison. There were three elephants at Belle Vue at the time. The third one was the African male referred to by Cornish.

Towards the end of his career at Belle Vue Lorenzo suffered two broken bones in his leg when another elephant panicked. It was Whit Saturday 1912. Lorenzo was working on elephant rides with keeper Stansfield. Lorenzo would be the senior keeper by a good number of years. There were two elephants on duty for the busy holiday. One of them, with about half a dozen people in the seats on its back, started to run. Something had alarmed the animal and, like the young Sally of years before, it ran to a place of security, its own den in this case. Stansfield, at its head, failed to stop it. Lorenzo, presumably with the other elephant, ran from behind. The young passengers were unhurt when the elephant reached its den. The broken bones in Lorenzo's leg marked the final year of his work at Belle Vue.

Maharajah himself had died in 1882 after ten busy years in Manchester. The official cause of death was given as pneumonia. He chose to die in the same year as Charles Darwin who had changed the whole world's attitude to nature by giving man and the other animals common origins and a comparable development.

The ten-year period during which Maharajah lived at Belle Vue was dotted with events of considerable significance for all animals including man. The world's wild horses, in particular, suffered irreparable catastrophes. In the year of Maharajah's walk, the London Zoo Quagga, whose photograph still exists, died. It was the last Quagga ever to be in Britain. Four years later, in 1876, another wild horse, the Tarpan, became extinct. The year 1881 saw brief gleams of hope. The great Natural History Museum opened in Kensington, and a Russian colonel named Przewalsky discovered a new species of wild horse in Mongolia. The horses were not plentiful and were due for extinction in the wild. Their genes were saved, however, by far-sighted individuals and zoos and Przewalsky Horses can be seen over a hundred years later in the protection of zoos and private collections. The Quagga, however, was destined for premature and complete oblivion. One year after Maharajah's death the last ever Quagga died in a zoo. The zoo people had not had quite enough foresight to counteract the unforgivable slaughter of the horses by people outside the zoo.

In America, too, during Maharajah's lifetime, you could take a special train out to the herds of bison and shoot as many as you could. It was a sort of pleasure trip. The Americans who shot the bison from the surface of the continent did not even know enough about them to get their name right. They called them buffaloes.

Maharajah's name did not disappear from the official Guide Books for many years. His mounted skeleton was displayed in the Belle Vue Museum. He continued to be the only animal constantly referred to by name. His skeleton remained in the Belle Vue Museum for fifty-nine years – as long as the Museum itself existed.

"Of the many elephants Maharajah was the chief" George Jennison was to write.

Chapter 8

The Place Resounds with His Fame

In 1899 a Manchester Guardian writer called Filson Young did a series of articles about Belle Vue. He called his series 'Some Beasts and their Keepers'. At this time Lorenzo had been at Belle View for twenty-seven years. Records suggest he had four elephants to look after; Sally, Dinah, and two very young ones named Macduff and Macbeth (known, predictably, as "the two Macs"). The elephants lived in the purpose-built brick house, only a few years old and built over "the most famous running track in the North". George Jennison was right about the running track. It had a glittering record, but its destruction shows the high status which the animals held. The elephant house in which they lived is the one which was to last into present living memory. It had three large moat-fronted compartments. The reporter interviewed Lorenzo in the elephant house itself, in front of Sally's stall.

The taciturn individuality of the older Lorenzo comes over quite strongly in the article, especially in the context of the writer's slightly flippant style. One has the distinct impression of two levels of gentle mockery, one from interviewer to interviewee, and the other in the opposite direction.

"His Brother's Keeper"

"Whether one studies a beast or his human attendant, one's thoughts revolve in much the same circle of reflection. Lorenzo (let us make haste to adopt the name that has flamed on many a show bill) is not an elephant – he is a man; but his long intercourse with the greatest of creatures has brought his nature into accord with the solemn harmony of theirs. Time with his drag of years contributes to the stateliness of Lorenzo's mental habit, and when one has started him upon some path of narrative or dissertation he is neither to be tempted into unaccustomed byways, nor hurried, nor arrested in his course. In his own good time he will lead you round the track of memory and show you the sights; he is no more to be disturbed by his audience upon that voyage than is his oldest elephant, once set forth on her circular walk of penny entertainment, to be deflected by the cries of her riders as they drum her unflinching hide. In the slow mill of his own mind he has ground up all his experience of life with the brute beasts into a kind of science – not a kind to be found in text-books, perhaps, but one that anchors him to an old philosophy. Probably he knows nothing of the Vendanta school, and yet he is a true, if a belated, follower of Vyasa. He seems to aspire to the perfect repose of the Vedantist, who found in the science that contemplates changeless things the only possibility of elevation beyond change; and, like him, Lorenzo closes the gates of his soul, recalls his senses within himself, feeds upon the past and future, and becomes absorbed in pious meditation.

I found him one afternoon seated on the hot-water pipes in front of Sally's cage, gazing at her in a kind of dream. It was a quiet day, and very few people were in the house; there was little or no business being done in bell ringing or sweet catching, and the two veterans gazed at each other across the bars. I hesitated to break in upon the silent duet with my foolish questions, but I was longing to hear the man talk about his charges. He gave me but little of the kind of gossip I wanted to hear; his mind was revolving questions of far vaster import; indeed, he almost resented my prying curiosity as to the private life of his beasts, and shielded them as though from the gaze of a mischievous busybody. What he did let fall, however, in the course of a few prefatory remarks (as to the nature of beasts generally), made before plunging into much deeper subjects, was profoundly interesting.

'Elephants are like people,' was his burden; 'show them much affection, and they'll take advantage of you when they can'. A cynic, you will observe, but it appears that he has excuses. There seems to be this great difference between the domestic as opposed to the wild animal – upon the one you may lavish affection and caresses, and he will love and respect you the more, but in the other, awe (which is the only really neutral ground upon which to make terms with a wild beast) and, in a less degree, affection diminish in proportion as you are demonstratively affectionate. We all know the man who must be kept at a distance lest he presume upon any little kindness shown to him; that is the wild beast. The dog or the horse is like a friend or good servant who knows how to value your civility. Approach an elephant daily for three months with loud words and an indifferent bearing, and he will like you and be very much afraid of you at the end of the time; feed him upon candy for the same period, treat him tenderly, and he will hold himself at liberty to stamp on you some day when he has nothing better to do.

There is something admirable in the austerity of such a bond as that between Lorenzo and Sally. They have known each other for nearly thirty years; for half of that time, I dare say, she has been his chief interest in life, and yet how few caresses, how few words even, have passed between them. Their mutual understanding, her loving, respectful dependence, his control, are alike perfect; although if he were not by and I were to enter her cage she would probably kill me, I should not be afraid to lie down in her path and let her walk over me if he were beside her. Not very much afraid, I mean. It is a constant effort, he told me, to refrain from petting so old a friend, and I can well believe it. He said, quite simply, 'If the animals were taken away from me, I think I should die;' but he is jealous of his influence, and makes the effort. From one or two stories which he told me I gathered that elephants are lovers of routine and resent any interference with their daily custom. For example, my friend was in the habit of taking one of his elephants every morning to the brewhouse, where the brute was used to have a drink of ale. For some reason, however (whether owing to the influence of some remote ripple of the teetotal movement or not I am unable to say), the practice was discontinued, and my lord arrived at the brewhouse one fine morning to find the door shut. Whereupon he raised a great boo-hooing, rushed through the gardens in an ecstasy of rage, and finally brought up in the middle of a lake bellowing and trumpeting as though to the Hades of the beasts. The sequel to this exhibition is significant of man's relations with his jungle captive. The keeper went up to the enraged monster with a piece of bread, and led him submissive to his den. Where bullying fails with a beast one may successfully appeal to his gluttony, and with these two weapons one is armed cap-a-pie against the lower creation. Here were several tons of brute beast rushing about in a frenzy because of a disappointed thirst, and the remedy for it all lay in the palm of a man's hand.

But listen to Mr Lorenzo while he communicates some of the riper fruits of his experience. 'It's all make-believe with animals. They think you're stronger than you are. It's your business to keep that idea going; if they ever happen to find out their mistake you've got to step out of the way to avoid trouble. It's astonishing how you can take elephants in. I can scare them as much with a straw as with a big stick. Their eyes magnify; they think the straw's a tree and that you're a giant.' This was evidently the starting-point of a loop-excursion from Mr Lorenzo's path of dissertation, for he diverged upon speculations. 'It's my belief, you know, that all our eyes magnify. We think things are bigger than they are. I don't believe it's as far from here to America as we think it is.' In my foolishness I suggested that the number of miles was known: and I have seldom been more confounded in argument than I was by his reply. 'Miles? What's a mile? I believe a mile isn't so long as we think it is, nor a yard, nor an inch. We magnify, and nothing's as big as it looks.' I tried to consider soberly upon this statement, but I felt the whole ground of my beliefs rushing past me and swinging into space. The more one thinks about it the more dizzy one becomes, and longs for some hold upon fact. Montaigne, perhaps, might have done justice to such a theme. I, however, had better leave the plain statement for your consideration.

But my companion gave me little time in which to exercise my amazed thoughts, for he was off again in a vein of reminiscence. 'You mustn't disappoint an elephant. I remember once, when I was with a travelling menagerie, we had an elephant that used to shift the tents and carts about when we gave a performance, and when the work was done they used to take him to the living van and give him a loaf of bread. I told them it wouldn't do. I said, 'Drop that, or there'll be trouble over it; I never knew any good come of coddling elephants.' Well, one Sunday morning we arrived at a village where we could get no bread; the baker's shop was shut, or something; and when the shifting work was done, off went the elephant as usual to the living van. Someone tried to stop him going, but he shouldered through the crowd in a way that meant business. When he found there was no bread he just took hold of that van and tipped it over and danced on it; and I guess there wasn't any less than fifty pounds' worth of damage done that morning. No, you mustn't coddle them.'

Mr Lorenzo was called away here to attend to the wants of some other of his charges, and I remained gazing at the monster before me, grim and grey like old Time – the very age of it made me tired. All round me, in the other cages, the business of feeding and cleaning was going forward; loaves of bread, enough to feed a multitude of men, were being wheeled about by the truck load and distributed amongst the eager animals. Truly, as Montaigne said, we are servants of our beasts; 'what carke and toile apply we not ourselves unto for their sakes;' a small army of men is paid to wait upon them and it is a kind of homage that one renders before their cages. Even those who come to scoff can hardly gaze for long at an elephant without being sobered and humbled. I was feeling very small indeed by the time my friend came back.

I was so fortunate as to stumble on Darwin's name during our conversation, and I fluttered it before him like a toreador's cloth. 'Darwin; ah! there you go; it's astonishing how ignorant people (no offence, sir) are misled by Darwin. Now Darwin was a very clever man – don't run away with the notion that he wasn't. But to my mind Darwin was a bit wrong. I've lived with animals; I know them; and I think Darwin got hold of the wrong end of the stick when he said we came from apes. Darwin said we've grown upward; I say no, we're growing downward.'

Let me say here that I do not hold myself responsible for any mistake I may make in expressing Mr Lorenzo's remarkable views. His language was at times obscure, and he refused to elaborate points upon which I would fain have been better informed. I do not myself pretend to understand his views, but one must accept them respectfully from so veteran an authority.

'Look at apes,' he went on. 'Do apes grow any more like men? If you go to Borneo you don't see men running wild in the ape forests, do you? I confessed that the phenomenon had not, to my knowledge, been observed. 'Well,' triumphantly, 'and if man came from apes. you'd see a man walk out of the forest every now and then, and him or no one else not know where he'd come from. No, sir, Man's growing downwards – downwards and eastwards.'

I staggered under the shock of this new complication. 'Eastwards?' I gasped. 'Yes, eastwards. The further East you go you see men more like apes and beasts; they've all been like us once, and some day we'll be like them, and we'll go on going down and be apes, and oysters too, before we've done.' I tried to lead him back to a less weird region of thought, but he had not yet finished. 'The human race is a wonderful thing. Men and women. It's my opinion women will be as good as men some day when they get more exercise.' The Downward and Eastward theory flashed a contradiction across my mind, but I did not interrupt. 'A man has lots of exercise, but what does a woman do? Nothing, but down on her knees beside a dolly-tub.' And he made an inimitable scrubbing motion with his hands in the air. 'I believe in bicycles,' he said; 'and they'll make women every bit as good as men some day.' The word bicycle sat awkwardly on the tongue that had uttered things so strange and deep; moreover, it spoke loudly of the commonplace. And I prefer Mr Lorenzo's conversation when it concerns his own familiar subjects; so, not without evident regret, he turned away from the promising field of generalities.

I heard but one more anecdote from him, and then he withdrew into silence like the fowl in a cuckoo clock when the hour has been proclaimed. He told me how he brought Maharajah, an elephant of wide fame, from Edinburgh to Manchester. When Wombwell's menagerie was dispersed, this elephant (one of the largest that has ever been brought to England) was purchased for the

Belle Vue collection. The keeper led him to the railway
station and embarked him in a great van; but the royal
shoulders were shrugged, and the top of the van came
off. 'We took to the road then and marched southward,
sleeping where we could.' I like the picture of great
Maharajah and his keeper "marching" along the wild
North road; one can almost hear the tramp and shuffle of
their feet, hour after hour, while the great and small
figures move over the rolling moorland and pass under
the silent, heather-clad hills. At one inn to which they
came the landlord, although doubtless a devout
Scotsman, refused to accommodate the behemoth, and
desired that he should be removed from before the door.

'A'll have no sic oncanny beastie aboot the place – tak'
it awa', mon.'

The keeper suggested the stable, but the landlord
snorted.

'Ye cudna get 'um in – tak' 'um awa'.' A gallon of
beer was bet upon the issue, and Maharajah at his
master's bidding knelt down and shuffled into the stable,
taking the door-posts with him. The landlord still
objected, but, said the keeper, 'Very well; I've put him in
– you get him out.' Mine host's authority failed him here,
and upon the bet being liquidated amity was restored.

Maharajah died of consumption years ago at Belle
Vue, but the place still resounds with his fame; the awe
in which he was held still lingers in the voices that speak
of him. Mr Lorenzo told me that I should find his
skeleton in the museum; and thither, having taken leave
of my friend and thanked him for his discourse, I went, as
to a shrine. I regarded, not without emotion, the vast
ruinous framework supported by iron girders in the
posture of life; I passed my hand over the great bleached
bones, and in fancy saw them clothed upon with a bulk
of living flesh. It is a strange thought, thus to make of the
dead his own monument; a strange event that this grim
creature, ravished from his far-off home to be a show for
multitudes, should even in death have the privacy of the
grave denied to his bones. There he stands, an outlined
mockery or a noble monument – which you will. But
even when his own fame is dead (and these bones shall
long outlast it) his huge ruins may commemorate the

prowess of Mr Lorenzo, his good friend and brother, when he in his turn shall have escaped from a derelict race that even now plunges downward and eastward to destruction.''

I feel no need to apologise for reproducing this piece unedited and in full. Filson Young was genuinely sensitive to the skill and experience of Lorenzo and the awesomeness of Maharajah, and, above all, to the relationship between the two. Although the writing is very much Filson Young, Lorenzo himself does speak to us. Lorenzo would have had little formal education and it is easy to scoff at his interpretation of Darwin. Suffice it to say that Lorenzo's reaction to Darwin was his own, and immeasureably more thoughful and considered than the reactions of many more 'educated' people both then and now. Lorenzo's theory does have a kind of logic in it, and it certainly obviates the need for all those interminable arguments about the Creation and the Fall. Lorenzo's thinking was ahead of Young's in seeing evolution as part of the here and now and the commonplace.

The interview is interesting from many points of view, including the absence of any mention of a toll gate. And how accurate was Lorenzo's forecast about bicycles!

Mr Young's piece about the Belle Vue Museum, by the way, was reprinted in the Journal of the Zoological Society of Greater Manchester for Winter 1987.

Chapter 9

Precedents and Echoes

The everyday events of yesterday give birth to the folk tales of today. The experiences of Maharajah and Lorenzo are a massive tribute to a man-animal relationship, but the experiences, the long walk, the unbreakable bond and the ensuing fame were part of an everyday job. The events took place within a tradition of walking between towns, at a time when a keeper's job allowed the right kind of man to devote his life to an animal which was probably held in affection, but not greatly understood, by the public. The walk and the bond, if they were unique, were unique only in their grand scale. The events were neither without precedent nor without subsequent echoes.

One such echo sounded briefly in South Africa. E. H. Bostock, who took over and then widened the range of Wombwell activities, sent a circus to South Africa. A seven-foot elephant bolted from Wynberg railway station. She ran the eight miles back to Capetown where the circus had been staying for some weeks. Pursuers on horseback were of no avail. She was eventually hitched to a steam tractor, taken back to Wynberg and put on a train without difficulty. She was later trained to assist in loading the menagerie waggons onto railway trucks and was the last animal to board the train.

E. H. Bostock himself had once purchased an additional elephant in order to impress a relative and rival. He bought the elephant from Mr Cross of Liverpool (he of the Edinburgh sale). The purchase was against the advice of his astute mother. The elephant was to travel by rail from Liverpool to Stafford, to arrive on a Saturday morning. It did not arrive in Stafford until Sunday morning at seven o'clock: it had refused to travel by rail. It had walked from Liverpool, tethered to a heavy cart pulled by three horses. He was tired on his arrival, but as soon as he had recovered he dashed out onto the street. Only Lizzie (of the burned back, and the killer of Stanton) was able to calm him temporarily. The young male was soon returned to Mr Cross. It is noticeable that in this incident there was no keeper with whom the 'troublesome' elephant had a relationship; no Lorenzo, no Scott to take the situation in hand.

The last of the Bostock & Wombwell menageries came to an end in Scotland, as did the first; this time in Glasgow. The year was 1932. The remaining animals included quite a few large mammals. Several Camels and two Elephants were in the group. How history repeats itself! The animals were bought en block by the Zoological Society of London for the new (and revolutionary) animal park at Whipsnade. The menagerie travelled by train from Glasgow to Bedfordshire. The train attracted great cheering crowds at the stations on its journey south. Carlisle, which had sheltered Maharajah for a night on his way south, had well over seven hundred people on the station platform to cheer the train. The Camels and the two Elephants, Dixie and Rosie walked from the station through the streets and along the lanes to Whipsnade Park. Exactly which station they walked from varies according to different reports. The present Curator at Whipsnade suggests that it was Dunstable North, on the evidence of photographic records. In this case, the distance would be only about three and a half miles. The parade also included a Giraffe, twelve Lions, Tigers, Leopards, a Polar Bear, Hyenas and Sea-Lions. This was a functional walk from station to park but was probably the last of the major British menagerie parades. Dixie's keeper was called George Braham. He refused to accept the sleeping accommodation found for him because he had always slept with Dixie. He was eventually persuaded to leave the Elephant for the night; the tradition was clearly not dead.

Dixie was not content with her quarters either, she was not at ease until her own, comparatively small, menagerie sleeping van was available to her, inside Whipsnade Park. She helped in the moving and lifting when the Whipsnade elephant building was under construction. Like Maharajah, she was to give rides to thousands of children.

The last of the Wombwell's menagerie waggons served as a group of temporary cages at Whipsnade. In the end, most of them went for firewood. Highway Elephants and menagerie waggons were no more.

L. R. Brightwell left a vivid word picture of the last stand of the waggons:

> "Before the lion and tiger dells and other features of the park were completed, these vans were drawn up into a hollow square, and with a canvas roof, made a quaint old-world spectacle throughout the winter on one of Whipsnade's lawns. Printed notices requested visitors to

refrain from smoking whilst in this straw-littered haven,
which had, as its centre piece, a huge fire roaring gaily in
a gigantic open brazier.''

Twice in its history Manchester has failed to support its
zoological garden – three times if we count the nineteenth-century
Aquarium in Whalley Range. Its museums, however, have fared
better. For almost the whole of their time in common, the
Manchester Museum on Oxford Road, in the middle of university
land, and Belle Vue, a couple of miles away, were happy to do
business with each other. One of the museum curators had been a
Belle Vue employee. Gerald Iles became the Zoological Director of
Belle Vue in 1933 when he was twenty one years old. He was a
forward-looking and ambitious young man who was to bring to the
zoo modern publicity and maintain its zoological prestige, although
many of its buildings were already a little neglected. He did not like
the Belle Vue Museum, however, nothwithstanding Maharajah's
skeleton. He closed the museum soon after he took over but it was
not until 1941 that he sold Maharajah's skeleton to the Manchester
Museum. There were three items in this particular sale and the
Museum offered £37 for the three; two pounds for a Capybara, five
pounds for an Anteater, both mounted, and thirty pounds for
Maharajah's skeleton. Iles' letter to Miss Legge, of the Museum,
dated 26th May 1941, contains the following paragraph;

"I am very glad the skeleton is remaining in Manchester,
it is a fine exhibition piece and will look well in your
galleries. I have a press cutting from the "Times" of
April 1872 which mentions that this elephant was
purchased from Wombwell's Menagerie for £680, so I
think you are getting it very cheap."

Nevertheless, he was glad to be getting rid of it. Maharajah's
skeleton was displayed, and still is, along with the small painting of
'The Disputed Toll'.

Meanwhile, Belle Vue's twentieth-century elephant keeper was
by no means letting the Lorenzo tradition fade. Of the more famous
names associated with the Belle Vue keeper staff (Matt Kelly and
James Craythorn, for example), elephant keeper Phil Fernandez was
by far the most photographed. In fact it was often rumoured he was
the most photographed man in Britain. Fernandez was a Malayan.
Like Lorenzo, Phil Fernandez tended the elephants and supervised
elephant rides. Probably unlike Lorenzo, and certainly unlike Scott,
Phil Fernandez always (and that means always) wore an oriental
robe around the gardens. Like Lorenzo, Fernandez had arrived at

Belle Vue with an elephant, in this case, Lil, a female Asiatic, in 1921. Fernandez brought Lil from the East. It comes as no surprise to learn that he had been working for Bostock's. Like Lorenzo, he became an elephant keeper after working with other species. He had the usual history of hair-raising experiences such as true animal keepers take in their stride (and which the phoney ones tend to seek out for the benefit of the media), including the skilful mercy-killing of a sick elephant with an oriental sabre. Lil died in 1947. She, like Maharajah, was taken over to the university. Her fate was not to be displayed; she was destined for the university department of anatomy. Fernandez became ill in 1956 and died in the November of that year. Like Lorenzo, he outlived his own special elephant and worked on, caring for others.

An actual sound echo of Lorenzo's fame must still be occasionally heard in a band composition by Dr Thomas Keighley, a musician and composer from the Pennine side of Manchester. Keighley entitled his piece simply 'Lorenzo'.

Maharajah was never Lorenzo's pet, never his accessory, never just a tool of his trade. Maharajah and Lorenzo were equals; separate and different entities brought together by fate and bonded together by mutual respect.

Maharajah's skeleton in the Belle Vue Museum

Indian Elephant at Belle Vue –
the keeper nearer the elephant would appear to be Lorenzo

Both photographs courtesy of Chethams Library

Appendix One

The Edinburgh Sale

The contemporary reports, from which these lists are compiled, contain a very small number of minor discrepancies concerning the price and number of certain of the smaller animals, and the occasional minor variation in the spelling of names.

The English and scientific names of the animals are those given in the reports.

Species	Scientific Name	Animal's Name	Purchaser	Price	Other
Racoon	*Procyon lotor*		Earl of Rosebery (agent)	£1.	
2 Agoutis	*Diasyprocta agouti*		Mr Bell, Langholm		10s each
Dasyure	*Dasyure viver*		Mrs Day, menagerie	7s	
Gennet Cat	*Gennetta tigrina*		Mr Jamrach, London	£1 5s	
Tasmanian Devil	*Diabolus ursinus*		Mrs Day, menagerie	£3 5s	
Diana Monkey	*Cercopithecus diana*		Dr McKendrick, Edinburgh	£7.	
Capucin Monkey	*Cebus appella*		Mr Rice, London	£1 10s	
Mandrill	*Cynocephalus maimon*		Mr Rice, London	£30.	
Mandrill	*Cynocephalus maimon*		Mr. Rice, London	£5.	
Anubis Baboon	*Cynocephalus*		Mr. Rice, London	£10 10s	
Anubis Baboon	*Cynocephalus*		Mr. Rice, London	£8 10s	
Hamadryad Baboon			Mr Jennison, Manchester	£3 10s	
Chacma Baboon	*Cynocephalus porcarius*		Mr Rice, London	£2.	

57

Species	Scientific Name	Animal's Name	Purchaser	Price	Other
Drill Monkey	*Papio leucophaeus*		Mr Jamrach, London	£5 5s	
5 Dog-faced Baboons	*Cynocephalus babouin*		Mr Rice, London	£3. each	
Black cat			Dr McKendrick, Edinburgh	5s	
Black Vulture	*Catharista jota*		Mr Rice, London	£3 10s	
Condor	*Sarcorhampus gryphus*		Mr Rice, London	£15.	40 years with Wombwell's
Emeu	*Dromaeus Novae Hollandiae*		Mrs Day, menagerie	£7.	
2 Pelicans	*Pelecanus onocrotalus*		Mr Jamrach, London	£6 15s each	Came from Earl of Derby
Scarlet Macaw	*Macrocercus*		Mr Rice, London	£3 10s	
Scarlet Macaw	*Macrocercus*		Mr Cross, Liverpool	£3 15s	
Blue and Yellow Macaw			Mr Rice, London	£4.	
2 Slenderbeak Cockatoos			Mr Rice, London	£1. each	With cage
3½ pairs Warbling Grass Parroquets (budgerigars)			Mr Rice, London	£2 2s each	With cage
King's Parrot			Mr Sanderson	£1 17 6d	With cage
Pennant's Parrot			Mr Jenkinson, Broughton Street	£1 10s	With cage
Rose-breasted Cockatoo			Mr Rose	£1 5s	With cage
Purple-capped Lory	*Lorius domicellus*		Mr Stewart	£2 10s	With Cage
Golden-headed Parroquet			Mr M'Gregor, builder	£2 10s	With cage
Indian Parroquet			Mr Peacock, Edinburgh	£1 10s	With cage
1 pair Lemon-crested Cockatoo	*Phyctolophis*		Mr Lindell, West Port	£2 14s	
1 pair Lemon-crested Cockatoo	*Phyctolophis*		Mr Jenkinson	£2 8s	

Animal	Latin name	Seller	Price	Notes
White-crested Cockatoo		Mr Dewar	£1 13s	
Lemon-crested Cockatoo		Mr Scott, Edinburgh	£8.	Good talker
1 pair Green Parrots		Mr Buist	£2 2s	
1 pair Rose-breasted Cockatoos		Mr Young	£1 10s	
Nylghau	Portax picta	Mr Ferguson (Van Amburgh's)	£26.	
Nylghau	Portax picta	Mr Jennison, Manchester	£10 10s	
Llama	Lama peruviana	Mr Jamrach, London	£15.	
Boomer Kangaroo	Halmaturus	Mr Rice, London	£12.	
3 Wolves	Canis lupus	Mr Bostock, menagerie	£1 12s each	
Ocelot	Felis pardalis	Mr Ferguson, Van Amburgh's	£6 10s	
3 African Porcupines	Hystrix cristata	Mr Ferguson, Van Amburgh's	£5 10s each	
Wombat	Didelphus ursina	Mr Ferguson, Van Amburgh's	£7.	
Leopard		Mr Simons, menagerie	£8.	Faulty
Brown Coatimundi	Nasua rufa	Prof Wyville Thomson	£1 10s	
Common Jackal	Canis aureus	Mr Simons, menagerie	£1 6s	
Saddleback Jackal	Canis mesomelas	Prof Edwards, Paris	£3.	
Thibetian Sun Bear	Helarctos tibetanus	Mr Jamrach, London	£5 5s	
Brown Bear	Ursus arctos	Mr Bostock, menagerie	£7.	
Leopard		Mr Jamrach, London	£20.	Performing
2 Leopardesses	Felis leopardus	Mr Jamrach, London	£20 each	Performing

Species	Scientific Name	Animal's Name	Purchaser	Price	Other
Hyena	Striata		Mr Bostock, menagerie	£3 5s	Performing
2 Wolves			Mr Bostock, menagerie	£1 10s each	
Lion		Hannibal	Mr Jackson, Bristol	£270	Male, black maned 6½ years old
Lion		Duke of Edinburgh	Mr Rice, London	£140	3 years old
Lion		Nero	Mr Rice, London	£140	7½ years old "very fine"
Lion		Wallace	Mr Rice, London	£85	7½ years old performed with Lorenzo in 'Androcles'
Bengal Tigress		Tippoo	Mr Jamrach, London	£155	3 years old, in cub
Lion		Boss	Mr Jamrach, London	£20	3 years old, 'faulty'; hurt eye
Lioness		Princess	Mr Rice, London	£80	about 3 years old
Lioness		Alexandra	Mr Rice, London	£80	about 3 years old
Lioness		Victoria	Mr Jennison, Manchester	£105	4 years old in cub to Hannibal
Lion		Prince Arthur	Mr Rice, London	£90	18 months old son to Hannibal
Lion		Prince Alfred	Mr Rice, London	£90	18 months old son to Hannibal
Leopardess			Mrs Day, menagerie	£6 5s	
Spotted Hyena	Crocuta Maculata		Mr Ferguson, Van Amburgh's	£15.	
Burchell Zebra	Equus zebra		Mr Rice, London	£50.	
Gnoo	Connochetes gnu		Mr Rice, London	£85.	

Animal	Species	Name	Buyer	Price	Description
Elephant	*Elephas indicus*		Mr Rice, London	£145	about 5'6" tall female re-purchase 'organ grinding and whistling, can travel 30-40 miles per day'
Elephant	*Elephas indicus*	Maharajah	Mr Jennison, Manchester	£680.	nearly 8 years old, male, tusked
2 Boa Constrictors			Mr Stevens, showman	£6. each	
Malabar Squirrel			Mr T Peacock, Edinburgh	£5.	
Bactrian Camel	*Camelus bactrianus*		Mr Morgan, Edinburgh	£19.	male, 12 years old 7' high
Bactrian Camel	*Camelus bactrianus*		Mrs Day, menagerie	£30.	female, in calf, 6' high, 10 years old
Bactrian Camel	*Camelus bactrianus*		Mr Edmonds, menagerie	£23.	female, in calf, 6½' high, 5 years old
Bactrian Camel	*Camelus bactrianus*		Mr Bostock, menagerie	£14.	male, 5' high 2 years old
Bactrian Camel	*Camelus bactrianus*		Mr Bostock, menagerie	£14	female, in calf, 5' high, 1½ years old
Dromedary	*Camelus dromedarius*		Mr Rice, London	£30.	male, 5 years old 7½' high
Dromedary	*Camelus dromedarius*		Mr Bostock, menagerie	£21	female, 6½' high 14 yrs old
Camel			Dr McKendrick, Edinburgh	£9 10s	male calf, born 6 Feb 1872
Spotted Carriage Dog			Mr Brown, gymnasium	£1.	
Indian Goat			Mr Liddle	£1. 7s	
Dog mastiff				£12	
Mastiff				£5.	
English Fox Terrier				£2 2s	2 years old

Poonah, the 3 year old Royal Bengal Tiger and mate of Tippoo, appeared in the sales catalogue described as ''magnificent'' and ''a splendid performer'', but died one week before the sale.

Appendix Two

The Dimensions of Maharajah's Skeleton in the Manchester Museum

The skeleton stands on a plinth which is 12 feet 2 inches long.
The overall length of the skeleton from tusk ends to tail can be estimated fairly accurately at twelve feet.
Both tusks, with the ends sawn off, are 28 inches long.

Tusk circumference at base: left: 13 inches
                             right: 14 inches

Tusk diameter at sawn-off point: left: $3\frac{1}{2}$ inches
                                  right: 3 inches

Distance between tusks at base (centre to centre):   13 inches

Top of Skull to ground: 7 feet 2 inches

Height of skull: 35 inches

Length of tail: 46 inches

Maximum height (middle of back to ground):   slightly under 8 feet

2 x front humerus: 34 inches

2 x rear femur: 38 inches

Existing top rear teeth: 6 inches long at base

Greatest width measurement (across backside):   3 feet 8 inches

Bibliography 1

Blunt, Wilfrid	*The Ark in the Park*
	Hamish Hamilton, London, 1977
Bostock, E.H.	*Menageries, Circuses and Theatres*
	Chapman & Hall, 1927
Brightwell, L.R.	*The Zoo You Knew*
	Blackwell, Oxford, 1936
Carrington, Richard	*Elephants*
	Chatto & Windus, London, 1958
Cornish, C.J.	*Life at the Zoo*
	Seeley, London, 1895
Frost, John	*A Survey of Elephants in Captivity in the British Isles*
	John Frost, Wallasey, 1987
Graves, Algernon	*Royal Academy Exhibitors 1969–1903,* vol. 3
	Henry Graves & George Bell, 1905
Huxley, Elspeth	*Whipsnade*
	Collins, London, 1981
Iles, Gerald	*At Home in the Zoo*
	W.H. Allen, London, 1960
Keeling, C.H.	*The Life and Death of Belle Vue*
	Clam, Guildford, 1983
	Where the Crane Danced
	Clam, Guildford, 1985
Mitchell, Sally	*The Dictionary of British Equestrian Painters*
	Antique Collectors Club, Woodbridge, 1985
Peel, C.V.A.	*The Zoological Gardens of Europe*
	F.E. Robinson, London, 1903
Schomberg, Geoffrey	*British Zoos*
	Allan Wingate, London, 1957
Silverberg, Robert	*The Dodo, the Auk and the Oryx*
	Puffin, Harmondsworth, 1973
Street, Philip	*Whipsnade*
	University of London Press, 1953
Wood, Christopher	*Dictionary of Victorian Painters*
	Antique Collectors Club, Woodbridge, 1971
Wood, Lieut.Col. J.C.	*A Dictionary of British Animal Painters*
	F. Lewis, Leigh on Sea, 1973
Young, Filson	*'Some Beasts and Their Keepers. I, The Wisdom of the Serpent' by "One of Their Friends"*
	The Manchester Guardian, 10 October

1899 reprinted in the Journal of the
Zoological Society of Greater Manchester.
Vol.4, No. 8 Winter 1987

Young, Filson   *'Some Beasts and Their Keepers. II, His Brother's*
Keeper' by "One of Their Friends"
The Manchester Guardian, 11 October 1899

Bibliography 2

Various editions of the following Newspapers were consulted, as well as the Belle Vue Official Guides for several relevant years.

The Bolton Chronicle
The Bolton Evening News
The Bolton Guardian
The Bolton Weekly Journal
The Carlisle Journal
The Chorley Guardian
The City Jackdaw
The Cumberland Pacquet
The Daily Review
The Edinburgh Evening Courant
The Hawick Express
The Kendal Mercury
The Kendal Times
The Lancaster Gazette
The Lancaster Observer & Morecambe Chronicle
The Manchester Critic
The Manchester Evening News
The Manchester Guardian
The Preston Chronicle
The Preston Guardian
The Scotsman
The Times
The Westmorland Gazette

Also, quoted in various of the above:

The Dundee Advertiser
The Field
The Daily Telegraph.

Index